MOORE RUBLE YUDELL

MOORE RUBLE YUDELL

A.D. ACADEMY EDITIONS • **E&S** ERNST & SOHN

ACKNOWLEDGEMENTS

Academy Editions would like to thank James Steele, the consultant editor for all his work on the monograph and recognises with gratitude the combined contributions of Charles Moore, John Ruble and Buzz Yudell in the preparation of this monograph. James Mary O' Connor has played a central part in its realisation and production, unfailingly providing assistance and encouragement to see it through several critical stages, as have designer Andrea Bettella and editor Iona Spens. We are grateful to Winnie Nielsen, Nanet Krogsbaek Mathiasen, Lotte Elkiaer and Jason Rigby for all their work on the design and to Andreas Papadakis Limited for their initial contribution.

First published in Great Britain in 1993 by
ACADEMY EDITIONS
An imprint of the Academy Group Ltd
42 Leinster Gardens, London, W2 3AN
and
ERNST & SOHN
Hohenzollerndamm 170, 1000 Berlin 31
Members of the VCH Publishing Group

ISBN 1 85490 183 4

Distributed to the trade in the United States of America by
ST MARTIN'S PRESS
175 Fifth Avenue, New York, NY 10010

Printed and bound in Singapore

CONTENTS

IN SEARCH OF SOMEWHERE
JAMES STEELE

At a time when architecture, in general, and firms in Los Angeles, in particular, seem to be polarising between iconoclastic individualism and humanism based on regional communal values, the office of Moore Ruble Yudell has become a prototype for designers with social sensibilities. From their first collaboration on the Rodes House in 1979, which was conceived on the kitchen table of a small apartment rented specifically as a base from which to carry out the commission, the three principals have produced a burgeoning body of work that is remarkable in both consistency of principle and client satisfaction. The ironic aspect of their having achieved such a paradigmatic stature is, of course, that Charles Moore, the initial generating force behind the formation of the firm, was himself once characterised as an iconoclast, now widely recognised along with Robert Venturi as a father of post-modern architecture. While the stylistic excesses of less assured hands eventually doomed that initiative, the basic human needs that brought it about in the first place have not diminished, in spite of the most determined post-structuralist attempts to intellectualise them out of existence.

Charles Moore is fond of telling the story of a lecture he once gave at a major university in Brazil, in which he criticised Post-Modernism as having become superficial and banal, with no real evidence of an awareness of history or context to be found in many of its highly publicised examples. He was interrupted at mid-point by one of the lecture organisers who told him how disturbed the students and staff were to hear all this, since they had invited him specifically because of his reputation as a leading post-modernist, to encourage those in the school who were then experimenting with the style, which they saw as being revolutionary. The anecdote is amusing, but also apocryphal, as an insight into the deeper reading that Moore, Ruble and Yudell can extrapolate from whatever surroundings they find themselves working in. These have now expanded to include commissions throughout the world. Moore's original stress on the idea of seeing architecture as a language that each practitioner must be allowed to speak freely has come under particularly heavy fire as being logocentric at a time when the purpose of symbolism, as well as memory itself, is being questioned. And yet, while the critical and theoretical skirmishes continue, the largely unrealised popular desire for each of these continues unabated, with very few architects addressing the issue of their existence. By doing so, this firm has managed to carve out a place for itself that has ensured survival and growth in the midst of severe economic vicissitudes that have sent many individualists diving for cover, until the patrons who sponsor wacky eccentricity can afford to build again.

The personal chemistry and design approach behind this achievement is elusive and difficult to analyse, and yet certain constraints can be identified, which have been frequently mentioned by the architects themselves. While they are notably uncomfortable with the idea of putting forward anything that even remotely resembles a proclamation or manifesto, they each recognise that their work is guided by an implicit set of operational principles. The first of these is a belief in collaboration itself, which is an extremely rare trait in a profession that has been conditioned, since Michelangelo carved his name on the Virgin's sash of the Pieta, to seek and value the personal statement above an anonymous team effort. The cult of the ego continues to be especially active in Los Angeles, making this determination to co-operate even more astounding. By taking a stance against the myth of genius – which reached its most recognisable form during the heroic period of the modern movement, but can be just as easily defined by many equally flagrant examples of arrogance throughout the city today – Moore, Ruble and Yudell continue to run counter to an attitude that is prevalent in the profession. However, there is a growing body of evidence that they have personally been instrumental in changing it. The Playa Vista project, which amounts to nothing less than a new town within the confines of the City of Los Angeles, is a perfect instance of such a change, since it is the product of a team effort between Moore Ruble Yudell, Andreas Duany and Elizabeth Plater-Zyberk, Moule and Polyzoides, Ricardo Legorretta and Hanna-Olin Landscape Architects. Each of the participants in this project – which promises to change the public perception of density, mixed use, and the predominance of the automobile – have been equally involved in all phases of its evolution with specific talents brought to bear where needed, but always subsumed within the social agenda involved. As such, the sharing of individual strengths is a legible extension of an identical process that takes place at a smaller scale in the Moore Ruble Yudell office itself, where interaction is spontaneous and complimentary; frequently compared by the principals to the kind of balance found in a jazz ensemble. As

Opposite: Tegel Housing, Berlin, Germany

Karow Plan, Berlin, Germany

Karow Perspective Drawing

Buzz Yudell has explained, in such a group, the musicians share a 'common theme, melody and approach to their art. Yet the process is informal and evolutionary enough to encourage, indeed to be dependent upon individual expression within this communal context. With a general sense of where they're headed, musicians take turns in the lead, interact and improvise as they proceed, and stimulate each other in a balance between individual expression and a common creation. Without a basis of shared beliefs and inclinations there would not be the energy of collaboration. Without the opportunity for individual exploration there would not be the possibility of discovery and evolution within the ensemble'.[1]

A second recognisable principle may be said to be a joint belief in a differentiating logic that underlies each project; not as specifically related to the contingencies of site, as it is to discovering the genus loci, or spirit of place that exists and bringing it forward in architectural form. Geometrical order is recognised as an indispensable and time honoured method of establishing this connection, but is not implemented in an overtly rationalistic or explicit way as a strictly physical diagram, rather being seen as the tangible charting of a mental map of sequences and experiences that are directly related to each place. This process, which is fragile and not dogmatic, gives each design an ineffable, narrative quality rooted firmly in the humanistic realm of space and time. It may typically begin with a tartan grid, and sequential patterns loosely based on the concept of the Beaux Arts 'marche', but eventually each of these is eroded, pushed and distorted by the tensions that inevitably erupt when systems overlap. Two clear examples of this erosion, that are totally different in scale, function and character are St Matthew's Episcopal Church in Pacific Palisades and Plaza Las Fuentes in Pasadena. The St Matthew's commission had originally been refused by several architects who felt that church conditions requiring congregational involvement in the design would be too restrictive. Moore, Ruble and Yudell, on the other hand, welcomed the opportunity to collaborate and after four consecutive workshops, they were able to identify several deeply held and often contradictory convictions about what the church should be. The heavily wooded sloping site, located below an imposing range of hills, presented another layer of possibilities which, in combination with congregational concerns, ecclesiastical conventions and local traditions, began to provide the architects with a framework in which to operate. The result is structured and recognisably liturgical and yet also extemporaneous and innovative, woven carefully into the grove of trees around it, with a series of courtyards and arcades imperceptibly shepherding movement towards an octagonal narthex in preparation for entrance into a breathtaking central space. There, the familiar question of how to resolve the forced centrality of the Greek cross plan, which has

historically been dealt with in countless ways, with mixed degrees of success, is answered in a new and refreshingly simple way, revealing the spatial possibilities inherent in the qualitative order that the architects refer to.

Because of its larger scale, commercial purpose and urban context, Plaza Las Fuentes demonstrates this order in a completely different way, and yet after careful study the same approach may be seen to be involved. The romantic faux-churrigueresque presence of the Pasadena City Hall nearby is the intentional focal point of the scheme, which opens up to it with a wide court meant to extend the axis of its tower and to encourage a pedestrian link between the two. An existing church on one side of this court helps to mediate between the imposing scale and intricate detail of the City Hall and the new architecture that answers to it, adding civic texture to the ensemble at a critical corner of the scheme, where the City Hall axis and 'Paseo' spine of the fountain-lined plaza intersect at a right angle. These fountains, which give the project its name, are magical, serving as a low screen wall between public and private space. Their sound, movement and reflection, which vary in a series of configurations, effectively activate what might otherwise have been a rather imposing extended elevation along the paseo; especially after sunset, when the massive walls of the hotel and office building across from the church seem to dance with constantly changing patterns of light. The 'marche', in this instance, has also been purposely interwoven between fountains, panels of grass and covered arcades to join all three in the mind's eye and make them memorable in a way that never occurs in more formal, symmetrical schemes. The final impression is one of historical and spatial continuity between the City Hall and the Plaza, civic grandeur of a kind not seen in American urban design for generations, and a studiously playful approach to the design of the ground surface that makes it all work in a delightful rather than deadly serious way.

Perhaps more than any other project to date, Plaza Las Fuentes also highlights the issue of 'place' which plays such an important role in the design approach of each of the principals and which is expressed most eloquently in Charles Moore's landmark article 'You Have to Pay for the Public Life'. While the ideas expressed in that statement have not received as much attention as Robert Venturi's *Complexity and Contradiction in Architecture*, which was written at exactly the same time, they are equally profound and insightful, with implications that have proven to be remarkably prophetic. The diminished public realm in the United States and the gradual loss of communal greens, squares and parks that have symbolised the democratic spirit since Lexington and Concord is nowhere more evident than in Los Angeles, which had precious few to begin with. In what is certainly the only city that has ever covered over an entire river within its boundaries with concrete, public space has never been a priority, with the freeway unexpectedly assuming the function of the place where everyone in the city meets, whether they want to or not. Recreating this lost realm, or establishing it *de novo* as an alternate to the California car culture is tricky business, especially since social patterns are in continuous flux and malls as a typical destination of a freeway journey seem to have now become a permanent fixture in the national consciousness. Recent initiatives in downtown Los Angeles, however, indicate that all this is now changing and the advent of the Metro may mean that the freeways' days as the predominant means of transport may now be numbered. The search for the appropriate formula for public space has now begun in earnest and Moore Ruble Yudell have helped undeniably to provide direction for it, since it has been one of their basic concerns from the start. Plaza Las Fuentes is significant in this regard, not only because it is in an urban context and seeks to re-establish pre-existing patterns and connections using a historical language, but also because it has always been intended to be commercially viable and so has adapted many of the proven techniques used by large-scale, indoor retail developments so that they will benefit the city, as well as the tenants. In the process, many of the preconceived continental configurations praised by Moore in 'The Public Life' and other publications since, have been tried and found wanting, victims of the same social changes that have doomed their charming but equally anachronistic counterparts in Europe, as well; all leading to a fresh look at what makes public space viable and lively in the 'edge cities' of the twenty-first century. [2]

While conscious of such social transformations and committed to determining what their appropriate expression might be, it must also be emphasised that Moore Ruble Yudell continue to believe in the existence of timeless ways of building that speak to the deepest aspirations and sensations of the people that these buildings serve. To find them, they try to identify commonalities between successful examples of architecture that effectively connect with their setting and accurately mirror the sense of shared experience in the public realm. This mixture of timelessness and evolution, as well as order and erosion, is also evident in three other recent projects which are all carefully adapted to the land: Tegel Harbour near Berlin; the Potatisakern in Malmö, Sweden; and Kobe, Japan. In each case, similar considerations, best described by the architects as 'a passion for making places of habitation', which are served rather than dominated by geometrical order, can be identified; as can the differences one might

expect in such widely dispersed cultural backgrounds. None of these employ literal references to historical prototypes, yet each is distinctly and unmistakably influenced by its particular location, while sharing a contrapuntal attitude towards open space. Without urban boundaries of the kind that have generated the Paseo in Pasadena, each of these return to the even more elemental question of the point of demarcation between architecture and nature, of deciding what is inside and what is outside and how that difference is dealt with. The ability to capitalise on it while weaving both together, to provide surprise and delight over and above organisational demands that must of necessity be different from those used in the city, has been a distinguishing feature of the work of this firm.

The Hua-Dong National University Master Plan in Hua-Lien, Taiwan is one of the latest and largest examples of the ability to achieve this delicate balance. Located in a valley between a coastal plain and the central mountains of Taiwan, the University accommodates eight undergraduate and graduate schools of engineering, arts and sciences with the auxiliary facilities they require, serving a student population of ten thousand in a village-like setting. Like Kobe, the scheme is organised around an axis extending from the mountains nearby, which is then used as the course of a meandering series of lakes and ponds. But here the spine generates a procession of open courtyards and widens to mark specific places such as the central plaza and the student union, while contributing to the system of campus flood control. In addition to establishing a more intimate, almost residential scale, courtyards are environmentally sound in this region, providing shade, shelter from frequent typhoons and protection for trees that are planted there.

The similarity of scope and variety of contexts represented by this brief selection of larger projects from the firm's oeuvre, make further comparisons of them a beneficial way of determining an overall, theoretical position in terms of 'placemaking', regional expression and the appropriate function of tradition in architecture today. Like the architects themselves, however, their work finally resists categorisation and is best appreciated and understood when approached without the preconceptions that typically accompany considerations of stylistically based directions.

Notes
1 Moore Ruble Yudell, *Architecture and Urbanism*, August 1992, p14.
2 A term coined by Joel Garreau in his book, *Edge City: Life on the New Frontier* (Bantam) 1991.

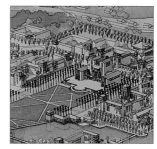

Hua-Dong National University, Hua-Lien, Taiwan

Hua-Dong Master Plan

ARCHITECTURE AND FAIRY TALES
CHARLES MOORE

This talk is based first on a series of recollections, of the feeling I used to get from John Lawrence, who for years in his very gentle way made me feel that it was right and necessary to think the thoughts and design the buildings that seemed to me to make sense; even when they seemed eccentric or altogether irrelevant, not what people were doing. It is also based on something Lou Kahn said when he gave the first John Lawrence Memorial Lecture here three years ago, and it is based most recently on six weeks in Rome – which is almost half enough time to make it seem possible to restore magic to its rightful place near the heart of our world. It was of that – the magic – that Lou Kahn spoke at Tulane three years ago:

> It's the fairy tale that is so important. I know if I were to think of changing my profession at this moment I would think of one thing – that I would love to write the new fairy tales.

Of course, he did, in his buildings, make magic and write architectural fairy tales at a time when the world most desperately needed them. I hope you won't think it too presumptuous or too academic if I try tonight to describe what I take to be the realm of the architectural fairy tale; or, at the very least, attempt to establish that there is such a realm. It is the realm, I think, of immeasurable dimension: of insides bigger than the outsides, of edges near the centre, of places where the familiar rules are for a time suspended. A characteristic of great fairy stories is that the quite carefully established dimensions of everyday reality open up magically – like the back of the wardrobe in which the children hide in CS Lewis' Narnia chronicles, or like Alice's famous looking glass. Both open up in an everyday way to a surprising new world of incalculable dimension. Perhaps closer to our everyday experiences (since few of us have such wardrobes) are the magically dimensionless breezes which come sometimes into our familiar world from a mysterious place that may be far away or may be very near. These breezes suggest the presence nearby of infinity. I think it is that nearbyness of the magic and the infinite, from where the breezes blow and onto which the openings open, that we care about. It is the infinite toward which the water flows, the time in which time has been curiously transmuted.

My real concern, though I will talk a little about real fairy tales, lies with the composing of architectural fairy tales – of the kind that Lou Kahn was talking about. I would like to consider how to make the tales that matter, without changing profession.

I am not, let me quickly say, trying for a general Procrustean-bed-like theory of architecture which would subject all buildings to a fairy tale test. However, I do think that the almost complete absence of that mysterious other immeasurable dimension in twentieth-century architecture, which has thrown that important part of our lives into the really quite limited realm of Walt Disney, makes ours a drearier world. Very probably, it would be just as bad to have an architectural literature that was all fairy tales, as it is to have one with no fairy tales at all. But we don't, I think, need to make that choice. The words are difficult and dangerous to use – semiologists have been poking the ground around us with pitfalls – but allow me to try to make some distinctions.

The architectural fairy tale is not fantasy in the sense that word is generally used, when it figures in situations in which the architecture of reason is pitted against the architecture of unreason – the rational against the irrational. Architectural fairy tales would then be expected to fit on the side of the irrational. I wouldn't like to categorise them that way, since I can't imagine how anybody could design a building irrationally. It takes some kind of reason to make any decisions at all, and I don't think that the people who claim some kind of late Teutonic logic behind their work have been doing work more reasonable than the rest of us. There is, however, the realm of fantasy in which some have worked, or at least sketched; but I don't think that is the realm of the fairy tale either, since fantasy seems to be something which starts and stays separate from the possible, from our real lives. The fairy tale doesn't. It partakes of myth, surely. But perhaps myth is a bad word. It is usually used in titles like 'Exploding the Myth of Soviet Supremacy' – as something that you are meant to do away with if at all possible. What fairy tales do, and why they are especially interesting to me and to many people who make architecture, is to start from the familiar: from the familiar wardrobe whose back opens to let you into a land from which you can just about always return in time for tea. Meanwhile, whatever span of fairy tale time has elapsed, there is a beginning and end in the familiar and even in the cosy.

I am not trying to enlist everybody whose work I mean to describe in the camp of the fairy tale makers, although I am mostly going to be showing the things that I believe partake of what I regard to

Bramante, Il Tempietto, San Pietro, Montorio

Thomas Jefferson, University of Virginia

Opposite, from above: Monte Alban, Oaxaca, Mexico; Sea Ranch, California, Charles Moore

be the positive qualities of the fairy tale. I don't know whether Mr Jefferson would have been pleased to be considered a fairy tale narrator with regard to his architecture or not, but he is my starting point, for the little house to which he brought his bride through the famous snow storm at the beginning of his habitation of Monticello is really the essence of house. The little familiar cottage became like the wardrobe, the kernel and the beginning for the grand extrapolations that marked the buildings and re-buildings of decades later, that for Thomas Jefferson became a life-long passion.

All the time (not just once upon a time), people built castles, which really do look like good solid castles capable of providing a base to dump boiling oil, to expel dragons and able to do all the things that should be done from castles. Those castles are part of a story that also includes cottages. In the story you have to go from a humble cottage to the castle. Then after you have been in the castle, perhaps for decades, you get to go late in the afternoon back to the humble cottage.

I have no limiting definition of the realm of the architectural fairy tale. What I have done instead, because such things must come in sevens, is to select three wonders, three yearnings and a surprise, as realms wherein the architectural fairy tale can fit. The three wonders have titles: they are called 'Intro-ductions', 'Obeisances' and 'Suspensions'. Before I introduce the first, I think it is worth considering the manipulation of all of them – not so much in our standard architectural terms of composition or putting things together to look at from some external point of view, as of choreography: of arranging, in this case, the familiar and the unfamiliar in ways that make sense of both, without losing the wonder of surprise and delight. I have been working in Rome on what I call the 'Doctrine of Immaculate Colli-sion', which I can't yet make work. The idea is that two things – the familiar and unfamiliar items that are waiting to be choreographed – can collide, smash into each other, and that what remains is the shape of a wonderful new architecture. The immacu-lateness comes when the pieces that have collided, or have been overlaid or jammed together, aren't destroyed by this act, as railroad cars are when they engage in the same action. Both remain whole, but the collision forms new shapes full of surprises and powerful things occurring. So in this choreography of the familiar and unfamiliar, an important act is the introduction of a set of pieces very like the castles and cottages I have described.

I think it is extraordinary in a time as complex as ours that most architecture around the world is still based on columns and on walls. I used to regard this as an interesting but probably irrelevant historical note. However, I have come to believe increasingly that in this powerful ancient pair of forms, the stuff that magic is to be made of still remains; the carefully proportioned, related and considered col-umns of a Greek temple have provided the pieces from which architecture is made, ever since they were developed. Thomas Jefferson's University of Virginia is a campus made with columns, large and small, pitted against one another and choreographed to move in stately ways up and down the lawn. Together with walls, either powerful enough to keep things out, as at Carcassonne, or just suggested, as in a graveyard in the California Mother Lode, the columns constitute just about the whole architec-tural world.

With just those pieces made by columns and walls we can introduce choreography of the familiar and unfamiliar. One such piece is the porch like the one on a fire station in Auburn, California, which has perhaps got out of hand and become more important than the building behind it. But it still serves as a powerful introduction, so that if there is magic in that garage (which I doubt), it has at least been properly introduced.

The wonders that lie behind the doors of San Zeno in Verona, more likely to be magical, are also introduced by a set of pieces quite standard for that part of the world: a porch of columns on lions' backs with a little roof over to make what Aldo Van Eyck would call the in-between realm to prepare you for the excitement of two really mysterious and wonder-ful doors, and then for the church itself.

There are doors as introduction, too. An example in Korea illustrates a gateway that is not properly part of a wall, but is made movable so that if the Chinese come you have the chance to cart the entrance south. I am delighted that the owners of the door should have shown a proper appreciation of magic to know that the door, the portal that invites one into and introduces one to their realm, is indeed so important that it should be carried away when it is time to flee.

There are enclosures of other kinds as well. A wall at Katsura Villa separates a portion of the outdoors on one side of the opening from the portion on the other side. Going from one space to the other is made an intensification of excitement, mystery and magic. The great shrine of Ise in Japan has as its most prominent feature a wall that affords only glimpses of a very remote building nearby. Mysteri-ous temples to which access is forbidden to most people lie just the other side of the protecting wall.

Enclosures are just suggested at Wies Church. Here, paired columns and some plaster hoopla over them make an inner shell that creates a second layer of enclosure more special than ever an inner-inner space. In Sir John Soane's house in London, a thick wall with mirrored reveals makes the transition from outside to inside much more important and gives further enclosure and importance to the inside.

In the first of my dirty tricks I juxtapose myself and Bramante. Encapsulation of enclosure to create a special introduction to a place happens in his Tempietto in San Pietro, Montorio. Similarly, in a recent house of mine in Florida, a little gazebo is placed inside a jungle-filled courtyard in order to

Opposite, from above:
*Guimares Castle, Portugal;
Gateway, Korea; Aviero,
Portugal*

13

Villa d'Este, Tivoli, Rome

*Shower, Orinda House,
California*

protect it from the winter winds off the Gulf. In each instance, the temple gazebo peg is shaped differently from the hole it is in, so that the tensions between the item encapsulated and the capsule intensify the sense of enclosure. In Bramante's case, the original intent was to surround the Tempietto with a bagel-shaped courtyard in which it would fit without tension. Luckily, for what I take to be the magic, this was never built.

The second of my wonders is 'Suspensions': of various things – gravity, time, or of the rules. Suspensions too often get passed off as mannerisms or mannerism; as some sort of freaky inversion in the mind of the architect who is simply trying to show his smart-aleck contempt for the system. I think that showing-off isn't at all the main point in developing suspensions, but rather the achievement of a heightened awareness on the part of the on-looker or the participant; for instance, when he sees that a building like this one in the north of Portugal is strangely floating over the water, or that the Queen of Heaven and her attendants are shooting right up through the ceiling on the altar at Rohr, in Germany. Even if you sit or stand there in person and look and wonder, they hang invisibly. Although they don't ever actually make it through the roof, they very clearly could if they meant to.

Suspensions of time happen in curious ways and places. At Middleton Place near Charleston, a great deal of effort was expended to establish symmetrical land forms with a pair of butterfly lakes, requiring an enormous amount of earth-moving by hand and basket in the swampy South Carolina lowlands. But then on top of that quite rigid geometry, there grows a jungle of green things, with, in the right season, the incredible and very temporary blooming of the azaleas for a splendid but fleeting occurrence on a strong and permanent base; in rather the same spirit that causes flowers to be put for the day on the altars of Indian temples that have been there for millennia.

There are other suspensions in time that seem to me to have some magic in them: one is the Corn Palace in Mitchell, South Dakota which is, unaccountably, made of ears of corn. These get old, as ears of corn will, and the building is reconstituted in some slightly different way with new ears. Another instance is a pair of churches near Beaufort, South Carolina, which have many contradictions built-in. Presumably, the congregation already had the right hand one and then built the left hand one. Then, seeing they had both, they kept them. The new one is smaller but more solid, so each one has its own virtues, which I suppose are seen as creating a kind of desirable tension between old and new.

The same kind of thing happens at the Ise Shrine in Japan – except obtains there a more regularised way of copying and of timing the construction of a new temple, with the demolishing of the old one in twenty-year cycles.

There are also suspensions of the rules. At the University of Virginia, Jefferson brings you through a low porch, covered, in order to get you inside by way of a higher porch, really not covered which inverts your expectations, twists your mind, and makes a kind of magic at Pavilion IX.

A look down the long allée at Versailles towards the canal, causes you to suppose that because of the architectural frame of urns and regularly spaced trees you are looking at a flat parterre, and that the canal is therefore tipping-up. Then you think about it for a while and come to realise that even at Versailles the water doesn't tip that easily and you are caught in a wondrous paradox in which you have to decide for yourself what's going on, thereby becoming involved.

My third wonder I shall call 'Obeisances'. One of the things that people do in fairy tales is go off to pay their respects to somebody. Witness, for instance, the crowd that sings 'We're off to see the Wizard' in *The Wizard of Oz*. It is an elitist scene going to see the Wizard that way – or the king, or princess, or whomever. However, it always seems to work out well: the recipient never seems at all ashamed of receiving into the royal midst the troop of small children, who are typically the obeisances, and generally letting them take over the kingdom or whatever seems suitable; so that a kind of democracy ensues, however hierarchic the beginnings.

There are, of course, also architectural places which are based on obeisance: a Bavarian altar or a temple with a place to get near it to make obeisances, as at Ise. I think there is great wonder in pavilions too. I have been noticing in Rome that on the skyline there is another part of the city above the part that's packed with people and rooms: the skyline is sprouting with little pavilions, above the Forum of Trajan, for example. Inside John Soane's house in London, a saucer dome with light coming in around the edges in the breakfast room is employed to make a special place, an aedicula, a gazebo – a place that you know is more important and good, more magic than anywhere else around.

And over time that sense of specialness stays with a great many aediculas. The tomb of Akbar in Sikkandra is composed of lots and lots of four-pillared aediculas, each surmounted by a little dome. Included here is an illustration of a former shower of my own in which I sought to enshrine myself while I was getting wet.

Little gazebos used as garden houses maintain an air of importance; as in the Farnese Garden on top of the Palatine Hill in Rome, or in the solid pavilion in a fountain at the Villa d'Este at Tivoli which you can't even get inside. However, the sense of its specialness, its capacity to have the world pivot on it is undiminished.

Edges, too, are places of obeisance; of the presentation of oneself to what lies beyond. I use as an example the edge of a park in Rome, and the edge of a garden with a pool in a house that I designed recently in California. The latter garden has a framing wall that reaches across a corner of the pool. This allows a special sense of separateness to be maintained from the not so wonderful view that lies beyond. The wall becomes an edge behind which your privacy is quite carefully maintained. Another edge is the bank of the Tiber in Rome. Again, a special Roman pavilion rides high above the Palazzo that lies underneath.

In a castle near Salzburg we find an edge to a lake, with a special gate. I don't know the circumstances under which you would open the gate, though I suppose you could open it in when the swan boat came by. However, the point is that it celebrates an edge between inhabitable land and the mysterious deep waters.

Windows as something that we think of looking in at function as the eyes of a building to give expression to it. But the act of looking out of a window is another part of its function. Kresge College at the University of California, Santa Cruz and the Nathaniel Russell house in Charleston, South Carolina, line themselves up, getting organised to face the outside which lies just beyond, in another kind of obeisance. Buildings of all sorts and degrees of fanciness on many continents, organise and pull themselves together to face the world that lies in front of them. However poor and shrivelled their miserable selves are, as in shanties in Utah, they put on a face, cover as much facade as possible to help make a street, a place outside them where the public action can take place. A much grander example from Mantua does the same thing quite straightforwardly. It pulls itself up almost as if it were on parade.

A fountain, the Acqua Paola in Rome, does the same thing with even more mystery and wonder. As you look through the facade, you can see that is what it is – a facade where there's open space out behind the left hand window. So its air of presentation of obeisance to the space in front is undiminished by any enclosed space that is being sheltered.

The Santa Barbara Courthouse attends to, even insists on its own facade by carving into it, by making a curious three-dimensional, big-arched little doorway. Our own monumental Laundromat at Kresge College, like the Santa Barbara arrangement, slips around behind a facade that's standing to attention. These two examples are both thought of not as three-dimensional buildings, but as two-dimensional faces paying homage to what lies in front of them.

In addition to my three wonders, I have assembled what I am choosing to call Three Yearnings. The notion of yearning, of quest, is central to fairy tales. The main thing that people do in fairy tales is to go in search of something or somebody that has been lost, in order to restore it or them to the proper place.

Three particularly powerful yearnings seem to me to be the yearning for the depths of the sea; the yearning for the vast distances of time; and the yearning upwards, towards the infinite. We have been told, earlier in this century, that we don't care about things which are not rational or sensible. As the century wears on, I believe that it becomes more and more apparent that at least some of the time and for whatever reasons, we do indeed care about the yearnings which take us out of the claustrophobic confines of whatever boxes we have built for ourselves. It is the nature of water, I am told – and it seems to have been agreed upon for the past millennia – that any little piece of water in the world is related, in the minds of mankind, to all the water everywhere else in the world, so that if we can connect with it in our minds, then making the imaginary journey down to the bottom of the sea where mermaids are and where Endymion went is an inevitable and even easy trip. In order for that to work, a number of things have to manifest themselves clearly: the sources of water are important and the way it falls and runs; the edges of the body of water, so you connect with it; and the way it disappears. Then the islands in it and their engulfments, their disappearing into the mysteries of the deep, are all essential to give that sense of mental leaning out over, of connection, that enables the mystery to work for us.

At the Trevi Fountain the running and falling are especially interesting, dramatic and worth the look. The source manifests itself naturally at an oasis at Sidi Haarazem near Fez, or is recaptured in a man-made work such as a fountain in Seville.

The flowing of water from a source may take the mind's eye with it, in a village in the Cotswolds for example, in ways that an asphalt road would hardly ever do; while the actual motion of the water in this rill at the Villa Lante carries the eye and the mind along as well.

At the Villa d'Este, the water slides and splashes. Similarly, at our Lovejoy Fountain in Portland, the water makes its own complex shape as it goes over simple six-inch concrete steps, or as the water flowing is countered by water squirting back up or bouncing. The edge and one's own capacity to make connection with that edge becomes very important in various towns along the Italian coast. In one case, the central piazza slides down under the surface of the water, while around the little bay one can stand right at, and lean out over the navigable and (until recently) clean waters of the Mediterranean.

The disappearance of water, too, is of special interest. Thus, for millennia, people have designed special drains like this one in a Roman city in Morocco; or they have personalised the whole thing, as with a mouth at the Villa d'Este which gulps down a great flow.

Islands standing in the midst of the isolation of the water, and therefore very special places, have occupied the minds of humankind for a long, long time – forming the basis of many intricacies. They focus Japanese art and thought. They stay in the mind even as they allow defence, as at the island of Mont St Michel off the coast of France where an engulfment even more dramatic than the ocean's itself is achieved with quicksand.

Rill, Villa Lante, Viterbo

Drain, Volubilis, Morocco

Mont St Michel

Sven Markellus Crematorium, Stockholm

In Lisbon, at the edge of the river there are steps descending into it. Then at Queluz, near Lisbon there is a curious boat that seems to be about to sink into a very murky pond. Both these examples draw our imaginations into the mysterious depths.

Parallel to this yearning for the depths of the sea there is, at least in many people, a yearning for the depths of time, with a chance of finding things lost in time. A fairy tale goes back through time in some way that changes the standard rules of chronology. A city like Rome, too, is full of buildings that are busy changing the standard rules of chronology – that, as in Trajan's Forum, heap medieval forms on top of ancient forms, with modern forms on top, within, next to, around, on; so that a palimpsest, a collage of all these things is in front of your very eyes, all of it laden, to my mind, with magic.

There's a kind of peek-a-boo in a building near the Tiber that seems to have some ancient and some medieval pieces put together for heaven knows what purpose. However, the mystery of each piece deepens the mystery of the whole. In a town in the Apennines a building seems to have a wall that is marching to the rhythms of one drummer, and a roof which is marching to the rhythms of another. I take it as a good example of my 'Doctrine of Immaculate Collision' – there the pieces are collided, and just an attempt to trace the wonder of it all is enough to give one a sizeable journey in time, space and magic.

The following pair of places suspend the rules of time and give us a chance to move freely in it. Over the hill at Sven Markellus' Crematorium outside Stockholm, there is a grove of trees that suggests that the centre of everything is just out of sight. It fills us with wonder. Then in a window arrangement in Bologna, one quite urgent set of convictions about the making of form that was based on the arch is tossed aside by somebody wanting the window somewhere else; leaving not exactly magic in this case, but some very strange tensions between what is and what might be. What happens when the arch decides that it has been wronged?

I find recollections to be of very special interest these days, since for decades we have been told that it is wrong to suggest in the things we do some pre-existing things we like, since that isn't modern. That has left the whole realm of making some connection with the past (as I was noting before) to the Walt Disneys of this world, who make some very interesting things but rob us of a freer and more real chance to make those connections ourselves.

I don't know where Jefferson got his notion for Pavilion IX at the University of Virginia. Perhaps he wouldn't have admitted any connection with Sir John Soane. Ledoux certainly interested him. However, in his manipulation of the Pavilion's half-dome entry he was clearly recollecting a set of forms that led back towards Rome. In Rome, somebody, I suppose in the 1920s, made a wonderful facade that is based on some Renaissance recollections very much transformed. It starts up as paired columns which perhaps too soon are capped off in little temples; then the paired columns start up again way behind and come sweeping back out as if they had forgotten they had to support the facade higher up; then they go through quite a few subtle changes until they emerge triumphant in an arcade with a cornice through which they go on their way up to being tinier temples, which are probably chimneys as well. I think it contains just about everything that any of us ever tried to do with columns (as well as quite a few things that none of us ever attempted).

My office has been working on designs for middle-income housing in the outskirts of Williamsburg, Virginia. Some dwellings are combined into six packs (named in honour of Anheuser-Busch, the clients); some are based on the Charleston single house, with its end to the street and a garden beside in which a car can be parked, representing a proven successful way of coping with a pedestrian neighbourhood fairly dense with parking without undue expense. There is also another notion here recollective of Charleston, in which the houses face the street with gardens behind part of them. The cars vanish through an arch in the building wall, to be parked in a lot in the centre of the block – out of sight for the people who are walking or riding up and down the streets. I am pleased to think that the pieces of these houses are modern, if modern means that you can't afford to have anybody shape them, so that corner pilasters are made of plywood, etc. But I flatter myself that the shadows are Federal. (It hasn't been established yet whether they are because we haven't managed to get this housing built.)

But all this is part of an increasingly overt and for my part necessary attempt to make a connection backwards in time with the forms that are established as especially characteristic of a place – in this case Williamsburg. I believe their existence is an important part of the reason why the people who are meant to buy the houses have come there in the first place. Therefore, the importance of this local idiom seems to me to justify a more overt recollection than might be appropriate somewhere else.

Another yearning, let's call it deformation, is a more formal one that honours form by messing with it. In one Roman example it celebrates the half-dome by squashing it; in another it honours a non-existent pediment by carrying corners up into a dormer window each side, and inserting very strange little pieces of railing that almost recollect a whole shape that might have been there once, but wasn't.

Deformations of other sorts can be seen in a building in Guimares, in the north of Portugal, where a set of separate houses are made into one by a great flight of steps up to some entrances conjoined; or in the fenestration of the jail in the Santa Barbara Courthouse, where a kind of syncopated carrying-on is, I think, legitimately recollective of the simplicity of the forms that were there before the windows began to dance around on it.

My third yearning is for the upward and infinite.

The two are in some ways connected: a temple complex like the one at Monte Alban above Oaxaca, is on top of a mountain in the first place, then full of great flights of stairs up further. Sometimes you have to descend again, in order to give you the chance to climb yet again, so that you always have the sense of moving upwards in this already enormously high place, as a part of your use of the place – of your connection with it. Ascending a baroque staircase is a similar experience, although the decor is a little bit different.

In the Doge's Palace in Venice, you move up the stairway past a set of humanoids who welcome you onward, or perhaps threaten you a little from the top of the stairway. The stairs themselves are an important part of the choreography, as in the Wells Cathedral Chapter House, or in a more humble flight in Mykonos.

Towers express that thrust upwards in another way; perhaps one of the main reasons for their existence. There is surely no need to get to the top either of Michelangelo's Campidoglio, or of a church spire in South Dakota. They are there mostly to point up to the sky and act as reminders of our hopes for connections in that direction.

We wanted a tower at our Sea Ranch Condominium, but felt obliged to look for further justification. We therefore filled it with bedrooms so that we could afford the space; but what we really wanted was a tower, partly as a pin to stick the building into a slope so that it didn't seem to be sliding into the sea, and partly to suggest upwardness. The remarkable building illustrated here, which I will try to further the reputation of, was built in Rome in 1926. It has a tower, some towering chimneys and quite a few other things as well; including recollections of more places than I have ever heard of. It is part of two or three blocks full of buildings that look like that and are in the aggregate almost more wonderful than you can bear.

Although probably not the best examples to indicate the infinite – which Michelangelo made a point of going well beyond – this particular yearning can also find expression in the very careful making of some sort of order out of harmonic number systems, as Palladio did, or out of carefully arranged proportions as in the case of the ancient Greeks or the Italians of the Renaissance.

This brings us to my seventh category – that of Surprise. I think that the most efficient and most powerful tool that architects have to create surprise is the manipulation of scale, to allow the inside to be bigger than the outside to command your attention. Surprises of scale can make things appear much bigger or much littler than they actually are – or let them seem bigger in spirit or smaller in size, or vice-versa. For instance, a windowless building in a street in Guanajuato, Mexico is painted in such a way that it looks as if it was dropped there by some Martian giant child. It becomes a magic interloper, maybe from outer space.

Energised by its bright painting, a tombstone in a cemetery near Cuernavaca becomes at once a toy and a powerful and moving object with considerably more monumentality than most great monuments I have ever seen. Again, I include an item of our own – a wading pool at the Faculty Club, University of California, Santa Barbara. Here, littleness is sought after and a kind of intimacy which makes it important whether a bird hopping around in the gutter is fitting or not, or whether a ten-month-old child (about the biggest child that will fit in that gutter) is being accommodated, and how deep the water is as it splashes from the child over to the gutter – so your attention is pulled down to a fine scale.

Attention is drawn to a miniature in something like the same way as a cabinet that is in Biltmore House in Asheville, North Carolina. It is full of mirrors in very special places, so we do not know how extensive the little miniature landscape is. It seems enormous as it pulls your mind and your wonder into its interstices. The following are two more things which seem to me at once very small and very big: the tombstone, where the frontal screen establishes a psychic distance to the back block that fills it with the mystery of the infinite; and then Stratford Hall, which is really not a very large house as great houses go, but becomes at once a miniature and a giant thing, by its four-squareness and insistence on taking hold of the piece of ground.

The things I have been showing have, I hope, common participation in some kind of fairy tale, so they share mystery and magic. They partake of other things too, of course, and I want to say again that I am not trying to preach an architectural revolution that would require us all to produce unending architectural fairy tales, but I do think that it is time to reject the restrictions that have made us ashamed to do things with an element of mystery, that keep us out of that realm of the unknown. I think it is now time to overcome our feelings of shame about mystery so that we can explore this realm. It is, I believe, an important part of our own minds and of the world around us.

Edited version of the lecture from The John William Lawrence Memorial Lectures, *Tulane University School of Architecture, 1975, dedicated to Lawrence's spirit of prophetic concern for the future's heritage.*

Villa with tower, Rome

Windowless building, Guanajuato, Mexico

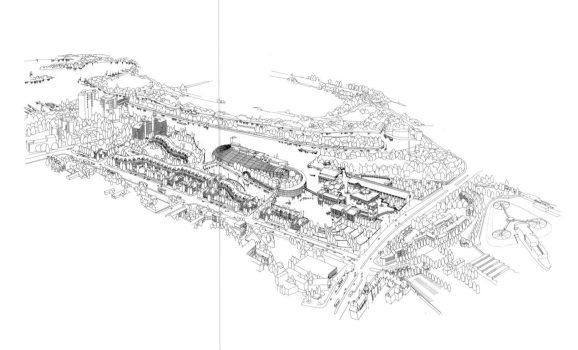

TEGEL HARBOUR: URBAN DESIGN FOR HOUSING RECREATION AND CULTURAL FACILITIES
BERLIN, GERMANY

Tegel Harbour connects a delightful suburban village with a chain of lakes and canals, as well as forested open space, providing Berliners with weekend outings, seemingly far from the city centre. The programme of this international competition, which we won in 1980, called for residential, cultural, and sports recreation uses. In response to planning guidelines, we were happy to make the three major components of the programme appear as discrete complexes on the forty-acre site. We wanted to make the harbour itself become a strong element in the plan, and therefore have extended the water dramatically into the site. Along the water's edge, a promenade connects all three complexes with the lake beyond.

At the centre of this new waterfront, the recreation centre takes the form of a small island or a great river boat, and contains an indoor-outdoor landscape of heated pools, waterfalls, beaches and gardens. One reaches this stationary vessel by bridges and smaller boats.

On the shore opposite, rows of houses slip gently in curved and straight lines parallel to the promenade, forming a series of broad-landscaped or narrow-paved edges to the waterfront. At the west edge of the site the row housing steps up to form a tower, identifying the new development from more distant viewpoints.

At the north-west edge of the site lies the cultural centre, whose broad sweep of steps and tower continue the urban character of Karolinenstrasse. The cultural centre also has its own waterfront entrance leading up to the plaza on which are placed a set of simple, almost industrial buildings. Various small institutions, such as a library, art gallery, theatre, and school are given well-ordered plans and classical elevations that have the feeling of waterfront warehouses.

The three complexes and the water come together at the entrance to the site, where radial rows of trees quietly draw the visitor down to the new harbour. The harbour expansion and public promenade were completed, along with the first phase of housing, in 1987.

Project: *Tegel Harbour Master Plan;* Owner: *Senator für Stadtentwicklung und Umweltschutz;* Design Architect: *Moore Ruble Yudell;* Principal-in-charge, Principal Designer: *Charles Moore;* Principal Designer: *John Ruble;* Principal Designer: *Buzz Yudell;* Project Manager: *John Ruble; Thomas Nagel, Leon Glodt, Regina Pizzinini, Peter Zingg;* Landscape: *Müller Knippschild Wehberg;* Structural Engineer: *Mannleitner Engineering Office;* Interior/Artwork: *custom design by Moore Ruble Yudell;* Colours/Interiors: *Tina Beebe*

AERIAL VIEW OF SITE

TEGEL HARBOUR: PHASE 1 HOUSING
BERLIN, GERMANY

This 170-unit housing complex forms part of our multi-use master plan, which was given first prize in a 1980 international competition. An additional 150 units within our master plan are being designed by other architects as a second phase of construction.

The housing area makes a rich and varied set of connections between Tegel Village and a small harbour, whose expansion and conversion to recreational use is also part of the master plan. Bounded on one side by Seventh Street, the housing begins with a series of bright villas, embraced by a second layer of gently undulating row houses. Within the row house sequence, our project establishes a courtyard with four 'houses' and four gates. The axis of this court proceeds directly through two of these gates to the landscaped commons beyond, ending with a view of the harbour. This visual axis to the water is seconded by a meandering path lined with tall poplars. In the great commons, the houses step up from five storeys to eight, plus a high zinc-covered roof. The roof is itself a lively village of dormer windows and loggiàs, set upon a more ordered base of stucco walls with precast pilasters and mouldings.

The social housing units are tiny, by code, yet relieved by generous loggias. Typical units allow views from their combined living/dining rooms to both the commons – to the south, and the harbour – generally north.

The design seeks to achieve an extraordinary degree of variety within a pre-cast concrete construction system, making this high-density 'townhousing' at once urbane and playful. All the units, popular locally, were rented well before construction was completed, in early 1987.

Project: *Tegel Harbour Phase 1 Housing;* Owner: *Beta Siebente* Design Architect: *Moore Ruble Yudell;* Principal-in-charge, Principal Designer: *John Ruble;* Principal Designer: *Charles Moore;* Principal Designer: *Buzz Yudell;* Project Manager: *Thomas Nagel; Leon Glodt, Regina Pizzinini, Peter Zingg, Eileen Liebman, Mel Lawrence;* Associated Architect: *Händel, Wolf und Zell;* Landscape: *Müller Knippschild Wehberg;* Lighting: *Richard C Peters;* Colour: *Tina Beebe*

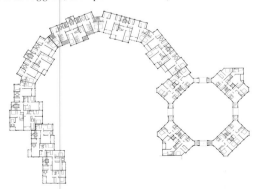

GROUND FLOOR PLAN

SOUTH-EAST ELEVATION

23

SOUTH ELEVATION

TEGEL VILLA
BERLIN, GERMANY

This multi-unit building is one of six – all designed by various architects to respond to our master plan and design guidelines for the Tegel site. They share the formal notion of a free-standing urban 'villa'; each one is influenced by its particular location within the plan. They play colourfully as 'signature' works against the more restrained baseline of the row houses.

Ours is adjacent to the entry plaza, and so it must make a kind of preamble to the rest of the project – which it does in two ways. First, it includes a small courtyard entered through a gate, hinting at grander courts and gardens to come. Secondly, it is somewhat over-articulated, using

formal devices which make sense only when they are revealed later in much larger buildings down the harbour.

In programme, our villa differs from the others: it is used for professional and doctors' offices rather than apartments.

Project: *Tegel Villa;* Owner: *Beta Siebente;* Design Architect: *Moore Ruble Yudell;* Principal-in-charge, Principal Designer: *John Ruble;* Principal Designer:*Charles Moore;* Principal Designer: *Buzz Yudell;* Project Manager: *Thomas Nagel; L Glodt, Regina Pizzinini;* Associated Architect: *Händel, Wolf und Zell;* Landscape: *Müller Knippschild Wehberg;* Colour: *Tina Beebe*

FRONT ELEVATION

HUMBOLDT BIBLIOTHEK
BERLIN, GERMANY

This branch library forms the first phase of the Cultural Center for the Tegel Harbour Master Plan. Its construction, started in 1986, coincides with the creation of a large water area adjacent to the harbour, plus a waterfront promenade and 350 units of housing.

The library forms one edge of the Cultural Center: its long hall continues the axis of the harbour, along the north boundary of the site. The view from the main reading room offers a forested landscape. Elsewhere around Tegel, the presence of industrial structures contrasts with well-preserved buildings in a range of nineteenth-century styles.

The industrial loft, carefully proportioned, became the prototype for our library. Its classical façade is broken with a glassy entrance bay, framed by a pair of free-standing portals. This leads to a central rotunda encircled by an arcaded balcony at the second floor. From the rotunda, a grand wall of books meanders along one side of the main reading room and gives access to the open stacks and smaller reading alcoves beyond. Passing continu-

ously above the various areas of the loft is a double-layer, vaulted ceiling lit by a clerestory window that throws light around and through the lower vault. On the north side, the light is balanced by a series of bay windows and doors that alternate with niches for books.

The steel and concrete frame is exposed on the interior. This industrial toughness is elaborated into a playful, almost baroque set of details for arches and ceiling. The book wall itself is, like furniture, composed of painted and natural hardwood. Exterior materials – metal sash, stucco and the standing seam zinc roof – combine with spare classical elements of precast concrete.

Project: *Humboldt Bibliothek (Tegel Humboldt Library);* Owner: *Bezirksamt Reinickendorf;* Design Architect: *Moore Ruble Yudell;* Principal-in-charge, Principal Designer: *John Ruble;* Principal Designer: *Charles Moore;* Principal Designer: *Buzz Yudell;* Project Manager: *Thomas Nagel; Leon Glodt, Regina Pizzinini, Renzo Zecchetto;* Consulting Architect: *Walter Hötzel;* Associate Architect: *Abeln, Lubic, Skoda;* Colour: *Tina Beebe*

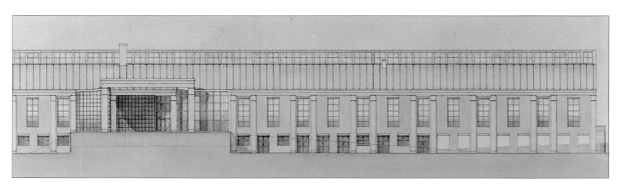

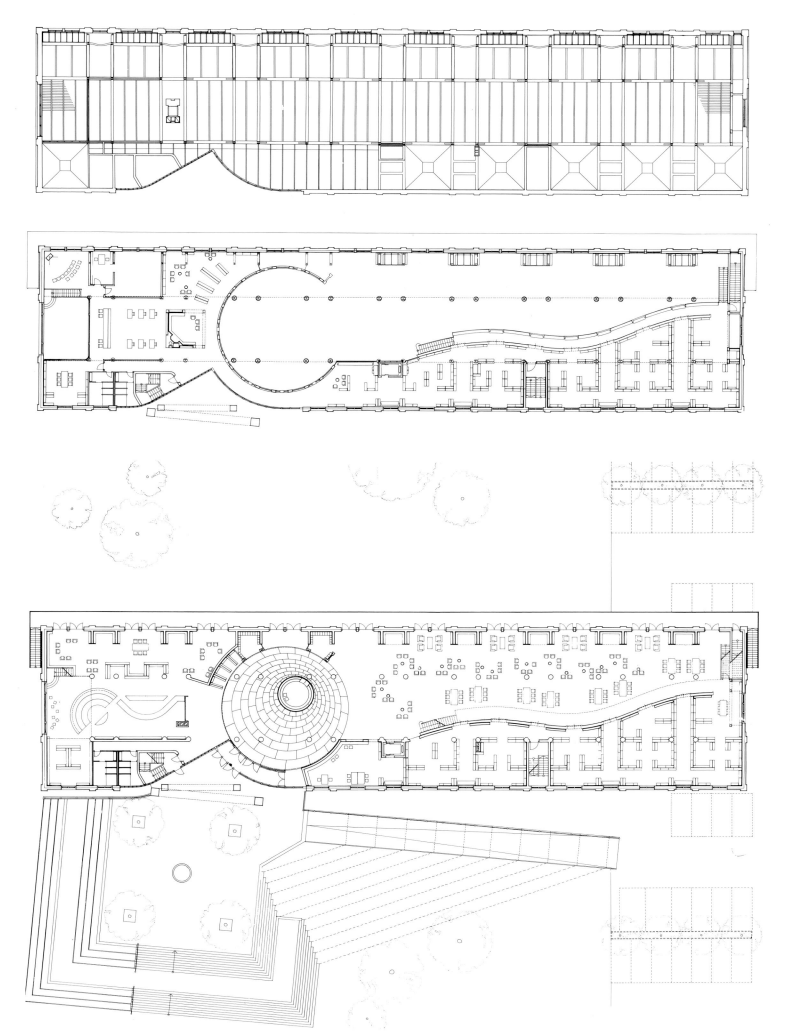

FROM ABOVE: REFLECTED CEILING PLAN; SECOND FLOOR PLAN; FIRST FLOOR PLAN

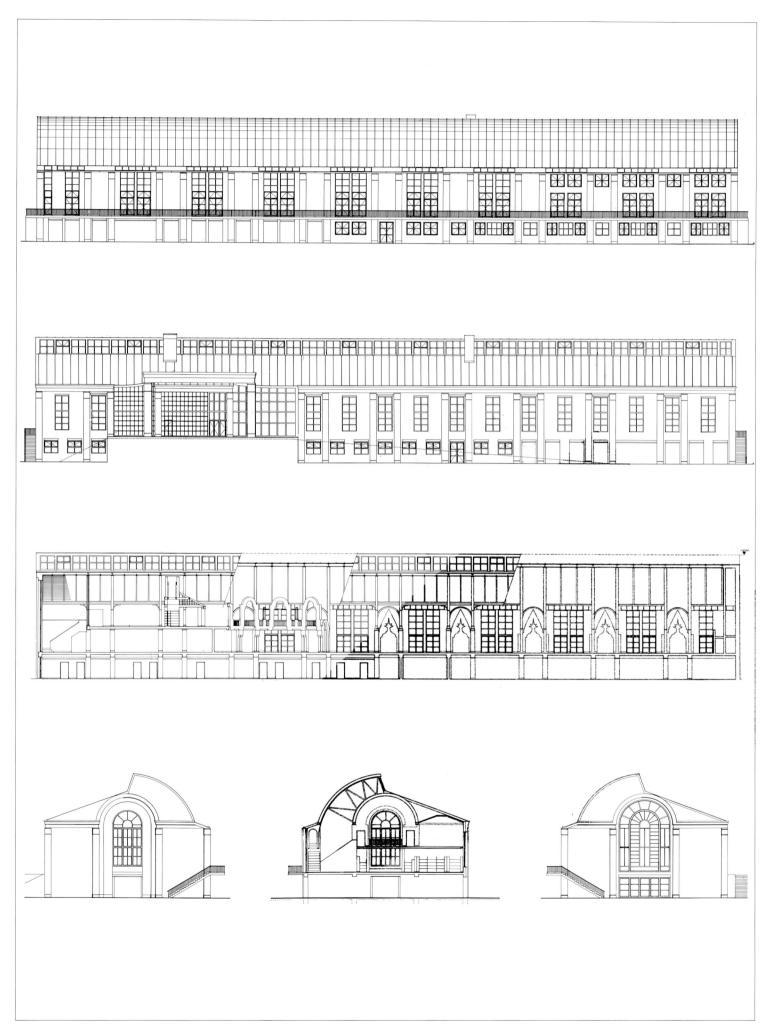

FROM ABOVE: NORTH ELEVATION; SOUTH ELEVATION; LONGITUDINAL SECTION; EAST ELEVATION, SECTION, WEST ELEVATION

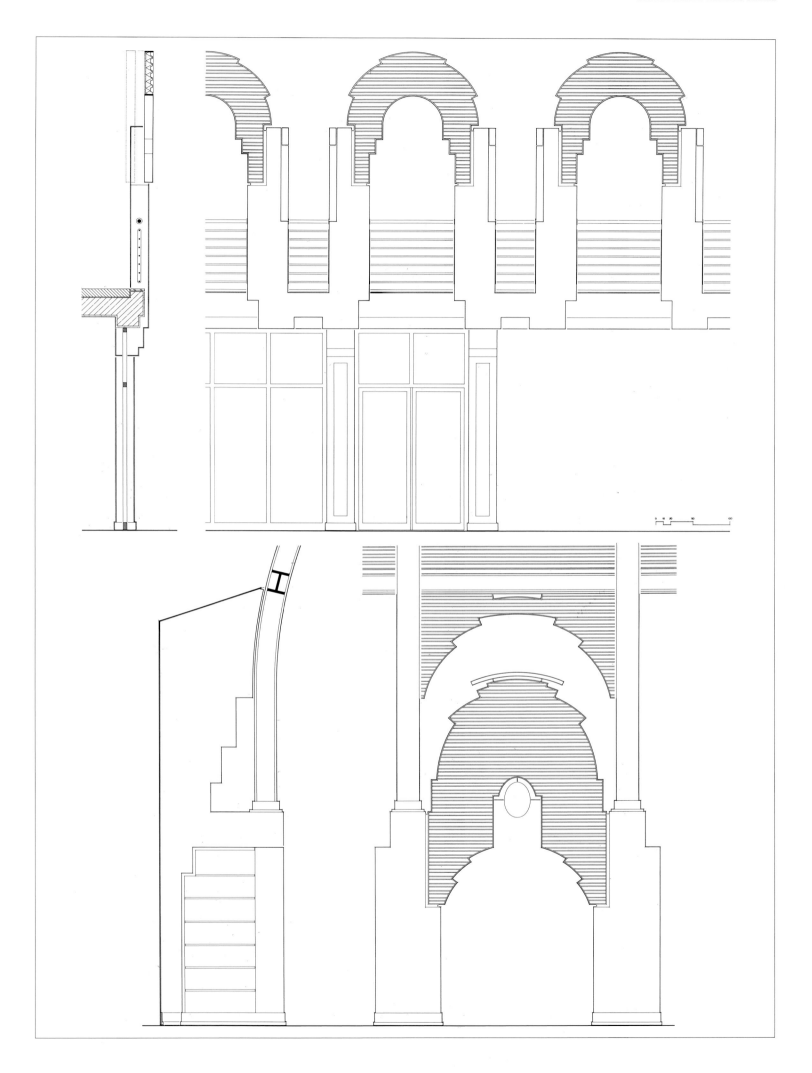

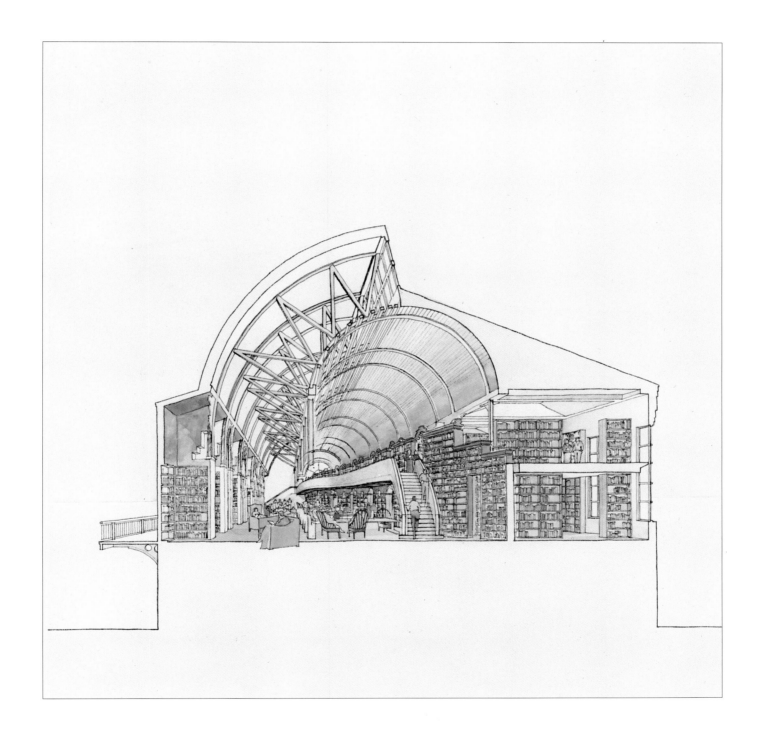

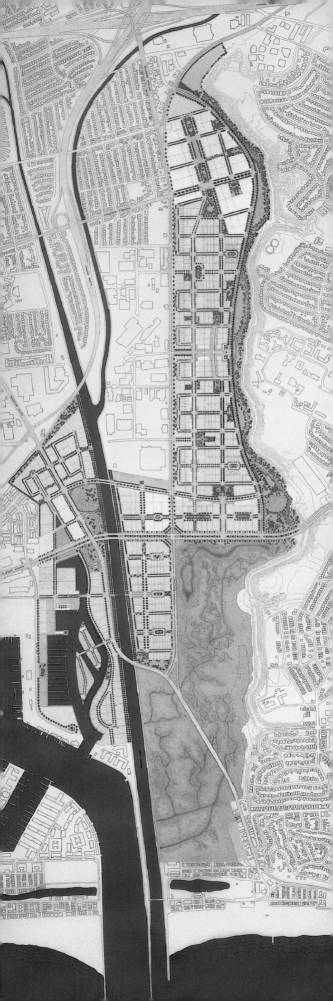

PLAYA VISTA MASTER PLAN
LOS ANGELES, CALIFORNIA

Playa Vista is a major new urban development encompassing nearly 1000 acres of largely undeveloped land at the heart of Los Angeles' Westside. In 1989 we were asked to participate in a team of planners and architects to create a master plan that would include include 11,750 units of housing, five million square feet of office space, 720,000 square feet of retail space, 2,400 hotel rooms and a forty-acre marina. Our challenge was to address social and environmental concerns within the economic constraints of our clients – to create an appropriate urban model for new development in Los Angeles.

Our first challenge concerned the notion of community: understanding what contributes to the sense of community in a place, and how traditional techniques and patterns of development might inform approaches to such contemporary issues – from public transportation to waste treatment and recycling.

We began by analysing California precedents for urban development in order to invest in Playa Vista the vitality and appeal of the best qualities of those places. Our strategy came to include a combination of traditional techniques, including mixed-use, mid-density, mid-rise planning, and the re-establishment of the importance of

civic and cultural amenities as essential elements of the community.

Over 270 acres of existing wetlands on the site are to be preserved. On the remaining land, an ordered system of blocks and streets – interspersed with parks, open areas and greenbelts linked by pedestrian paths – weaves the new community into the fabric of the surrounding city. Retail, civic and office uses are distributed among residential areas so that each unit of housing is within walking distance of transit, stores, schools, open space, or places to work. A diversity of housing types drawn from successful southern California precedents offers a range of choices for housing and includes approximately twenty-five per cent affordable units.

Owner/Client: *Maguire Thomas Partners*; Design Architect: *Moore Ruble Yudell;* Principal-in-charge, Principal Designer: *Buzz Yudell;* Principal Designer: *Charles Moore;* Principal Designer: *John Ruble;* Project Managers: *Curtis Woodhouse, Doug Jamieson; Mary Beth Elliott, Mark Peacor, John Johnson, Mario Violich, Linda Brettler, Craig Currie, John Taft;* Associated Planning Team Members: *Hanna/Olin Ltd, Legorretta Arquitectos, Moule Polyziodes, Duany Plater-Zyberk*

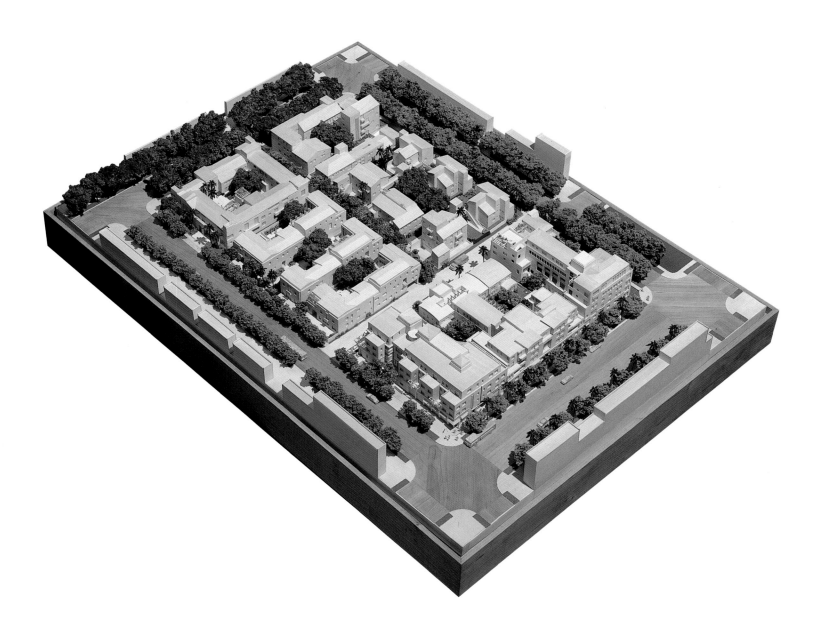

OFFICE CAMPUS PROTOTYPE
PLAYA VISTA MASTER PLAN

The Playa Vista Master Plan includes approximately five million square feet of office space integrated carefully into the fabric of the plan to provide tenants with a range of choices for the character, setting and location of offices. All locations are convenient to a range of amenities that allow a richer work-place experience.

The greatest portion of this space, approximately three and a half million square feet, is located at the eastern end of Playa Vista in a campus-like configuration. We were asked to develop a concept for a prototype office building that might occupy a typical block in this office campus.

The office prototype is composed of relatively simple elements combined to generate a rich and lively set of spaces as a whole. The plan maximises efficiency while developing a rich array of outdoor places – individual courtyards for auto arrival, as well as large and small courtyards for work-place interaction, cafés, and other shared amenities such as conference rooms. These spaces encourage a lively interior campus life, offering many choices for movement through the campus, both within the block and to adjacent neighbouring office campus compo-

nents. Close relationships are offered to district-wide amenities for the Office Campus as a whole.

A few carefully integrated special features such as gateways, corner towers, arcades, a central communal building and courtyards of varying size and character enliven the straightforward and economical diagram. Efficient and flexible floors are enhanced by rich views across terraces and landscaped elements. There is considerable flexibility in the size of individual lease areas – from smaller suites occupying one floor or less, to larger offices occupying the entire block of about 300,000 square feet. Upper level bridges make for easy connections among all parts of the project.

Project: *Playa Vista;* Owner/Client: *Maguire Thomas Partners;* Design Architect: *Moore Ruble Yudell;* Principal-in-charge, Principal Designer: *Buzz Yudell;* Principal Designer: *Charles Moore;* Principal Designer: *John Ruble;* Project Managers: *Curtis Woodhouse, Doug Jamieson; Mary Beth Elliott, Mark Peacor, John Johnson, Mario Violich, Linda Brettler, Craig Currie, John Taft;* Landscape: *Hanna/Olin Ltd*

KOBE NISHIOKAMOTO
KOBE, JAPAN

The fundamental principle of the project lies in making the closest connection to the landscape. The site, at the foot of the Rokko Mountain range, lies between the mountains and the ocean. It once possessed a rolling topography and a natural stream with water known for its quality in the making of Sake. This nine-acre area had since been graded and a series of block-like buildings imposed, which erased the sense of the natural topography.

Our master plan is based on the overlay of two concepts. A sense of the original character of the land is established by the creation of a 'natural' path – moving from a water source in the mountain garden, through the meadow garden and on to the ocean garden. This reinforces the mountain to sea relationship. The path is crossed by a formal axis of buildings and gardens which visually links the project to the city. The buildings along the natural path are shaped and sited more informally, while those on the formal axis are symmetrical. They vary in profile in order to meet strict Japanese requirements for natural light. Their collective character is resonant of mountains around a valley. The spaces between the buildings are shaped and detailed to be as important as the buildings themselves and to provide varied experience

for the inhabitants and visitors. At the intersection of the two paths a 'crossing' garden manifests a complex pattern of natural forms layered with symmetric geometry.

Project: *Nishiokamoto Housing;* Owners: *Mitsui Real Estate Development Co, Ltd; Haseko Corporation; Kawasaki Heavy Industries Ltd; Mitsui & Co Ltd;* Design Architect: *Moore Ruble Yudell;* Principal-in-charge, Principal Designer: *Buzz Yudell;* Principal Designer: *Charles Moore;* Principal Designer: *Buzz Yudell;* Project Managers: *James Mary O'Connor, Mary Beth Elliott, James B Morton;* Project Liaison: *Shuji Kurokawa; Go Miyashiro, Wing-hon Ng, Michihiro Ota, John Taft, Rebecca Kaplan, Eugene Treadwell, Arnold Swanborn, Ying-Chao Kuo, Doug Jamieson, Anthony Tam, Birgit Dietsch, Steve Gardner, George Venini, Duk Hwan Lee, Tony Tran, Gunnar Garness;* Landscape Team – Project Manager: *Daniel Garness;* Landscape Design Consultant: *Tina Beebe; Mario Violich, Akai Ming-Kae Yang, Cynthia Phakos, Heather Trossman;* Production Architect: *Mitsui Construction Co Ltd – Tamio Sanpei, Ryouichi Misawa, Satoshi Matsubara, Takao Ito, Mitsuru Nishikawa, Mitsuhiro Sugiyama; Haseko Corporation;* Landscape Production: Consultant: *Tetsuo Hanawa; Toyo Landscape Construction Co Ltd: Junji Yoshikawa;* Colour: *Tina Beebe*

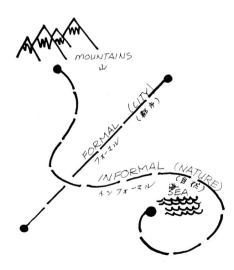

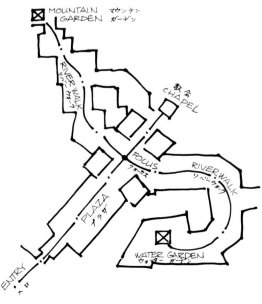

CONCEPTS AND TYPES OF SPACES

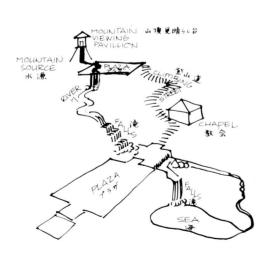

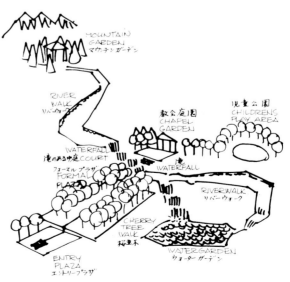

LANDMARKS AND LANDSCAPE

STAIR AND ELLIPSE LOBBY

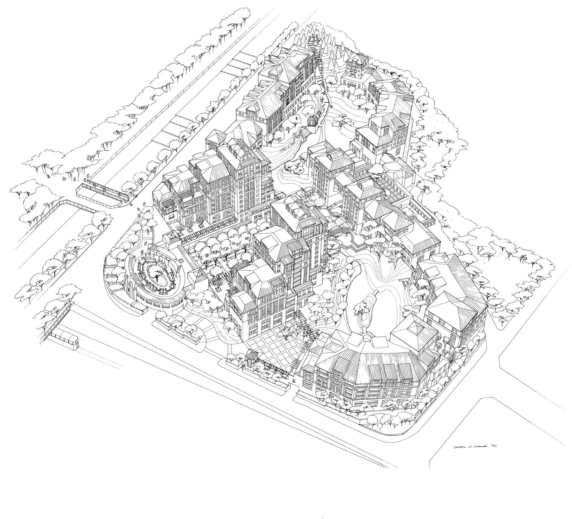

PREVIOUS PAGE: MEADOW PAVILION IN MEADOW GARDEN; *OPPOSITE*: LOBBY AND FORMAL COURT

BELOW: LONGITUDINAL SECTION THROUGH ENTRANCE HALL AND CROSS SECTION THROUGH ENTRANCE HALL

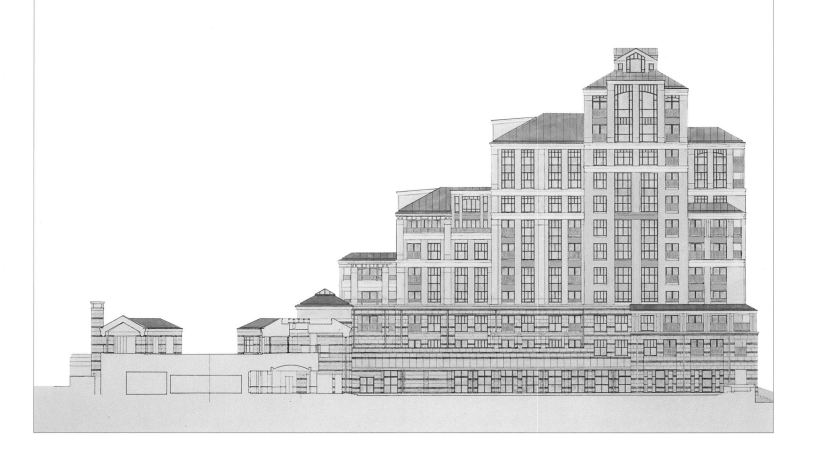

PREVIOUS PAGE: VIEW FROM SOMIYOSHI RIVER; *OPPOSITE*: ELLIPSE GARDEN ENTRY DETAIL

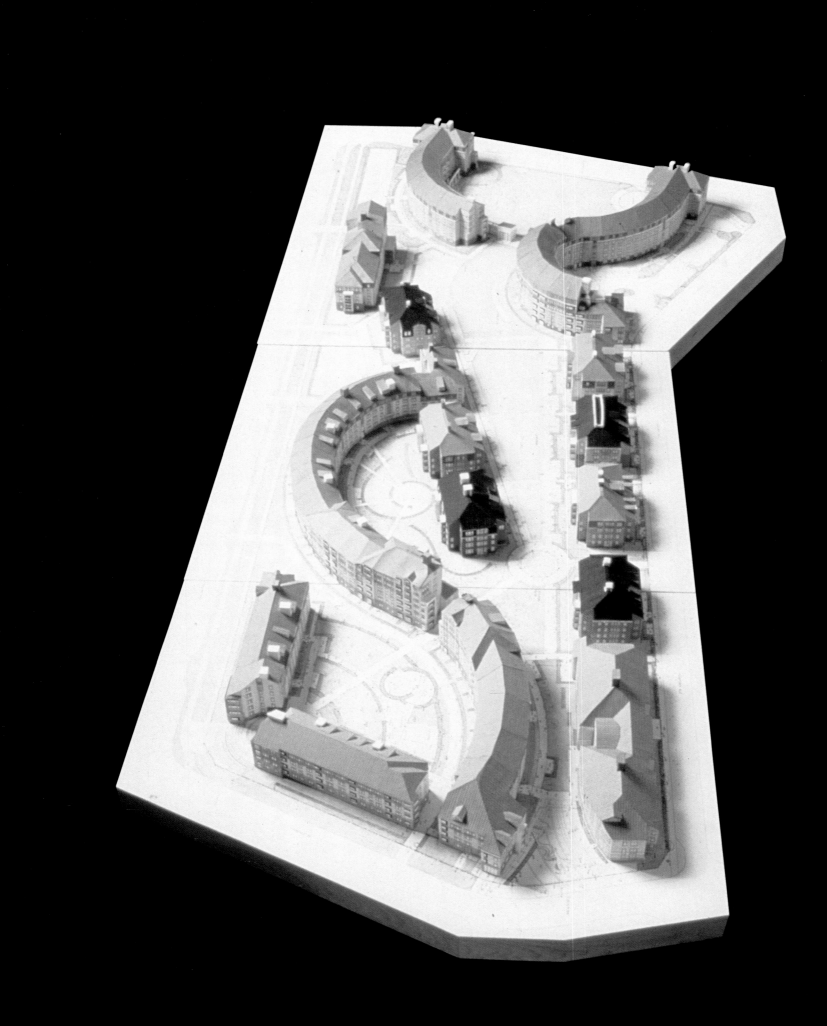

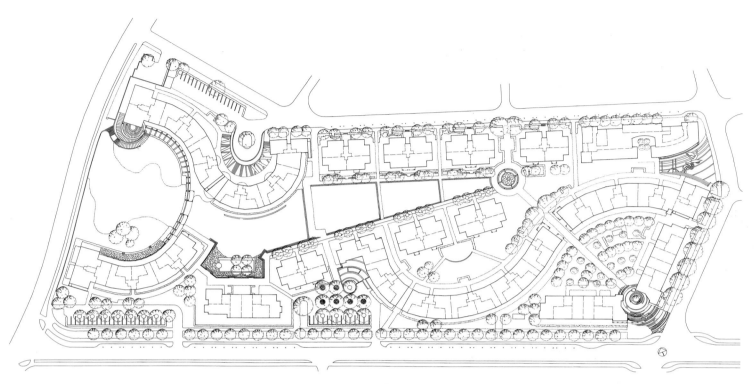

POTATISÅKERN
MALMÖ, SWEDEN

Along the Öresund (Golden Sound), which separates Sweden from Denmark, the city of Malmö owns a large tract of undeveloped land – until recently a potato field – in the midst of an established neighbourhood of older villas along tree-lined lanes. Our site plan uses the familiar housing types – villa and row-houses – to create a sequence of discrete landscape places linking the waterfront with the adjacent community.

The massing of the buildings is high enough to create adequate density, but sculpted down to a smaller scale where appropriate: at entries, at end, and along the street where the villas face the existing neighbourhood. The gentle meander of the row-housing is complemented by axial paths and vistas. A discrete set of traditional architectural elements – balconies, chimneys, winter gardens, pitched roofs, and arcades – unifies the buildings while allowing each villa to have a separate identity.

Materials are drawn from more traditional construction – metal roofs, sack-rubbed brick walls – to reinforce the consistency of the new buildings with their context. The sinuous curves of the 'snake' are rendered in subdued but warm tones to serve as a backdrop for the villas, whose colours are derived from the Swedish tradition of brightness, appropriate for Malmö's even light.

Project: *Potatisåkern;* Owner: *HSB Malmö; MKB; Skanska; Conatagruppen;* Design Architect: *Moore Ruble Yudell;* Principal-in-charge, Principal Designer: *John Ruble;* Principal Designer: *Charles Moore;* Principal Designer: *Buzz Yudell;* Project Manager: *Cecily Young;* Project Manager, Concept Phase: *Renzo Zecchetto; Ying-Chao Kuo, Chris Duncan, Tea Sapo, Yeon Keun Jeong, Mary Beth Elliott, John Taft, Tony Tran, James O'Connor;* Colour: *Tina Beebe;* Executive Architect: *Hultin & Lundquist Arkitekter AB, Malmö (Kurt Hultin, Dennis Johnsson) in joint venture with FFNS Arkitekter I Skåne AB, Malmö (Mats Jacobson, Bertil Öhrström)*

SITE PLAN

69

Building 'Q' South Elevation

Building 'R' South Elevation

Building 'R' North Elevation

Building 'G' North Elevation

Building 'F' North Elevation

Building 'P' North Elevation

Building 'M' North Elevation

Building 'N' North Elevation

Building 'O' North Elevation

ELEVATIONS FROM ABOVE L TO R: BUILDINGS 'Q' SOUTH, 'R' SOUTH, 'R' NORTH; 'G' NORTH, 'F' NORTH, 'P' NORTH; AND 'M' NORTH, 'N' NORTH, 'O' NORTH

Building 'K' West Elevation

Building 'U' West Elevation

Building 'T' East Elevation

Building 'S' East Elevation

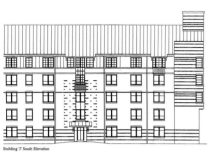

Building 'J' South Elevation

Building 'A-B' South Elevation

Building 'B' North Elevation

Building 'E' North Elevation

Building 'D' North Elevation

Building 'C' North Elevation

ELEVATIONS FROM ABOVE L TO R: BUILDINGS 'K' WEST, 'U' WEST, 'T' EAST, 'S' EAST; 'J' SOUTH, 'A-B' SOUTH, 'B' NORTH; AND 'E' NORTH, 'D' NORTH, 'C' NORTH

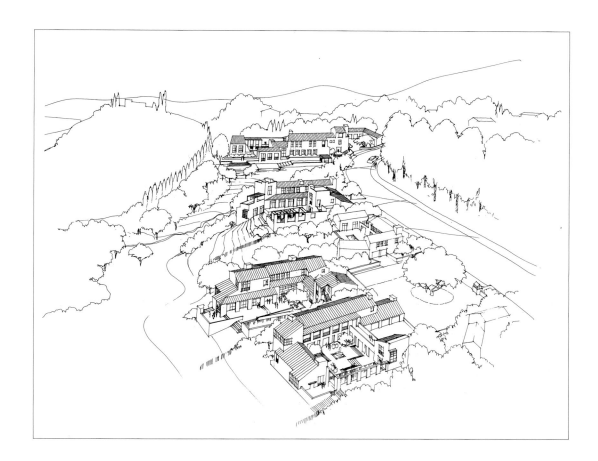

MALIBU HOUSES
MALIBU, CALIFORNIA

Several acres along a coastal bluff near Point Dume is the site for ten large single-family houses. Our client asked us to create a master plan and design four of the houses in a way that would give each house a distinctive character and allow them to work together as a unified composition.

The land rises steeply from the Pacific Coast Highway to a series of small ridges and canyons. Composed as a group, the houses are nestled along the ridges to take advantage of the commanding views while allowing each one privacy from its neighbours. Garages are grouped around shared auto courts. A common palette of colours and materials serves to unify the houses further, although they respond to their particular sites and orientation in distinctive ways.

The houses are made up of simple forms, articulated by sloping tile roofs, parapets, arcades, pergolas and bay windows. Each house, with its garage and pool house, is organised around an outdoor courtyard. This offers protection to the pool and outdoor living areas from the wind and frames the view beyond. French doors and windows work to break the distinctions between indoors and out.

Project: *Malibu Housing;* Design Architect: *Moore Ruble Yudell;* Principal Designer: *Charles Moore;* Principal Designer: *John Ruble;* Principal Designer: *Buzz Yudell;* Project Manager, Designer: *Daniel Garness;* Team Captain: *Akai Ming-kae Yang; Mario Violich, Cynthia Phakos, Tony Anella, Anthony Tam, Richard Destin*

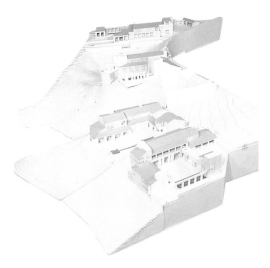

MODEL PERSPECTIVE; *OVERLEAF FROM ABOVE L TO R*: PLAN OF HOUSES 1, 5, 4 AND 2; HOUSE 1 MODEL

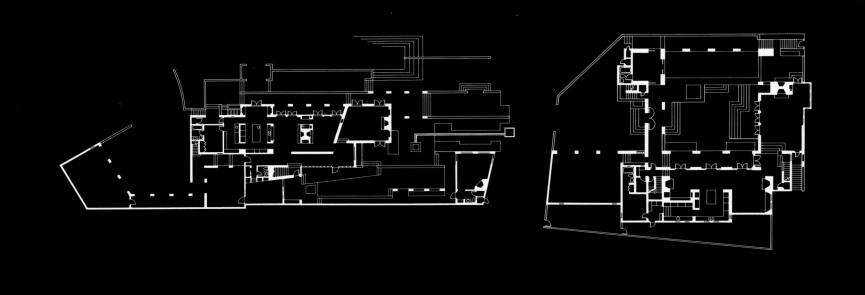

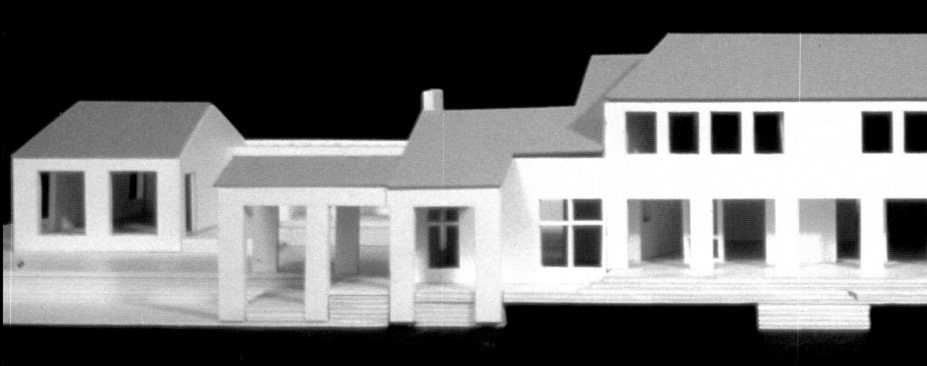

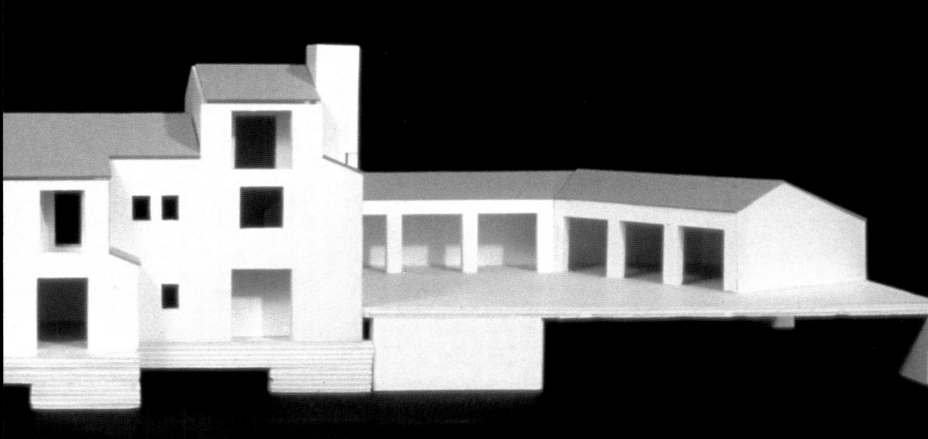

1992 WORLD COLUMBIAN EXPOSITION
CHICAGO, ILLINOIS

Working within a framework established by Skidmore, Owings and Merrill, Moore Ruble Yudell played a major role as members of a national planning and architecture team for the 1992 Chicago Fair project. Intended to be the first 'universal category' exposition since Osaka 1970, the Fair was envisioned to comprise some three million square feet of building area on a 575-acre lake-front site. Developing the 'Age of Discovery' theme, the site plan- *ning is strongly ordered in a series of water-courts, gardens, streets and waterfront promenades, providing a rich urban context for international and theme pavilions.*

Project: *Chicago World's Fair;* Owner: *Chicago World's Fair Authority;* Design Architect: *Moore Ruble Yudell;* Principal-in-charge: *John Ruble,* Principal Designer: *Charles W Moore;* Project Manager/Designer: *Renzo Zecchetto; James Mary O'Connor*

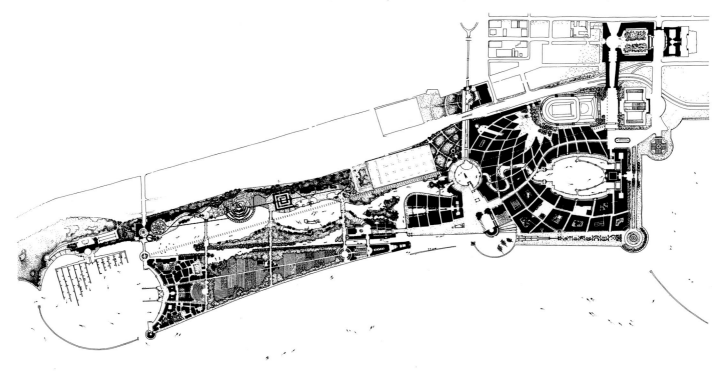

SITE PLAN

CHARLES MOORE
INTERVIEW BY JAMES STEELE

James Steele: Moore Ruble Yudell seems to be receiving many commissions abroad. How does the office approach them?

Charles Moore: There is a difference between designing in Europe and in the USA. There are all sorts of things that astonish me about going through our social housing when it is finished, like the dogs that people have. French poodles meticulously clipped, and the windows with huge cages with parrots and various exotic birds in them. I had a college roommate in graduate school who used to draw pictures of buildings with little children running around in front of them, carrying balloons, and I'll be damned if there weren't children carrying balloons in front of these houses. It was all perfect in a way that you could never comprehend. The whole business of living with, taking care of and seeing other people in public spaces, we have done just the way we do in our fixed renderings. I always thought that was some kind of joke, seeing a child in a rendering coming across a public space with a balloon in his or her hand. Then there's Japan, which is more curious. They're so excited about things being European or American that they don't want Japanese things. When working on the project in Kobe, if we proposed curved roofs they would say 'This is French'. I'd reply that it was Burmese, or Nepalese and they would say 'It's terrible'. Then I would say it was French and they would like it. So that was a problem because it's indicative of Japanese attitudes. But I don't know whether that's just my imagination or regional myopia. I do know that they didn't want it to look Japanese, Chinese or in any way Asian, and that is of course also a problem with the Germans who have particular ideas about what they want.

JS: There's a dichotomy, isn't there, in the fact that there's a global culture because of the speed of information. And on the other hand, people seem to want more identity than ever.

CWM: Well, I'm quite delighted for them to have more identity than ever. If I'm building in Berlin I wanted it to look like a building in Berlin. Did I ever show you Peter Blake's very nice letter?

JS: No. You've mentioned it but I haven't seen it.

CWM: I have a very nice letter from Peter Blake who said that he and I had had long arguments when I was at Yale about my negative notions of modern buildings and his positive ones. He reminded me of those and said, very nicely, that he'd been a resident of Berlin for much of his life and somehow we'd got our stuff at Tegel to look like Berlin. He said it looked great and congratulated us.

JS: This question resurfaces in discussions about traditional architecture and how it relates to context. Is this a process of osmosis? How does an architect achieve this fitting in, yet not fitting in? Being contemporary, yet relating to the past. Can it be done rationally? Is it just a process of study?

CWM: I'd like to think so but I'm afraid my own enthusiasms are altogether superficial and picturesque. I enjoy things that look like someplace. My own excitement is not about most people's ideas of vernacular architecture. But the vernacular apartments of Berlin, for instance, excite me and make me think that what I'm doing is something that has a Berlin look to it that I'm taking part in. Most of what is now being done in that culture is very superficial. I don't think it's particularly moral, or particularly immoral either. It's just a pleasure to contribute something real. When we're doing housing, people fuss about how we use paint to paint the entrances in patterns and colours that seem a little bit like old ladies who wear lipstick but don't get it quite straight. Yet that seemed to me to be very nice – a positive gesture that an old lady would put on lipstick even though it's crooked because she's showing that she is trying to pay attention to her appearance. I thought it mean of young architects to criticise us for putting paint on front doors, which is the same thing. It's somebody fixing up the public front of their house to make it look special, presumably for others as well as their own self-esteem. Having been brought up in the era when anything cosmetic was roundly deplored, I took some pleasure in gloating that cosmetics were a stripe of virtue.

JS: Speaking of cosmetics, I guess the one architectural style that has been associated with that is Post-Modernism, which you've been associated with in the past. Has that association been accurate?

CWM: I've got all sorts of feelings about that. I led a conference in Sao Paolo, Brazil, several years ago with a huge audience, consisting mostly of architecture students. I was giving a talk and making some

Opposite: *Kobe Nishiokamoto Housing, Kobe, Japan*

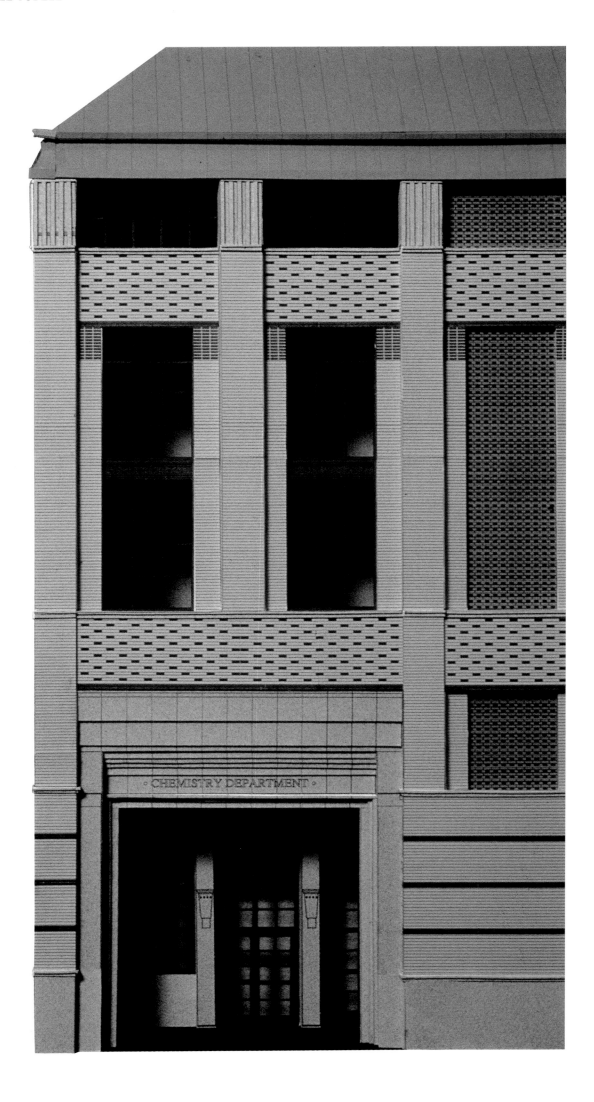

cracks about post-modern buildings that people were making and I was pulled aside by somebody who said, 'Stop it, you're the father of Post-Modernism. These kids have come here just as Brazil is getting over a heavy-handed dictatorship and are still required by their professors to do modern architecture. They're trying to do post-modern design and their teachers flunk them – so you represent freedom to them and you've got to stand up for it'. It seems to me that the post-modernists just stopped dead, got it all wrong and repeated the same old mistakes. What they were doing – that we're all trying to do – is to have some reference to things that we like and feel good about, that we are interested in associating ourselves with. The problems have been with detailing and empty surfaces, as in the worst of modern architecture; and with temples, extraneous arches and so on. The impulse to make things recollective of things we already like is strong and necessary – a complicated position to be in. People immediately fling the worst excesses into my face, most of which can be seen in LA.

JS: Is Post-Modernism giving this kind of recollection a bad name?

CWM: I don't think so. I don't know what to do about it except to just go ahead and be careful.

JS: When these kinds of things happen, as they did with modernism in third world countries that Peter Blake has talked about, they tend to overshadow any of the good work and delay revival of it for some period of time. This puts anyone dealing in that search in an awkward position, doesn't it?

CWM: I'm sort of pushing you farther back. Unless you're trying to do something altogether original and doing something never before seen on the face of the earth, you generally have serious mistakes.

James O'Connor: Today they call them cosmic beacons.

JS: The firm is well known for community design. Has that been successful in your view? Is it something that can continue, something that is feasible in today's society? Is it something that's viable?

CWM: I think so, and I can't understand why people don't do it more often. My standard excuse is that egos aren't big enough, and that you have to have more than the usual amount of self-confidence to be able to be open to coping with vicious tongues. But if you don't mind that and think you can deal with it, as I have always been able to, it seems to me a natural and reasonable thing to do. I like it because I'm always peddling things. I like getting an idea and trying to persuade a bunch of people that it's the idea for them. If it works out that they get the idea, or some idea, then salesmanship is not required.

JS: So if it doesn't revolve around one personality it is a process that can be effective.

CWM: I think so. It seemed to me that we were first doing it with St Matthew's Church twelve years ago. At that point I couldn't understand why everybody didn't want to do so. Now, I can understand better why, since it's a question of whether you'd lose a lot of money with a fixed fee structure. I'm still not sure it has to be that much more expensive to do. What possibly goes wrong is that architects are sufficiently uncertain about it all that they become defensive. For some time, the people who were supposed to be engaged in this process didn't know what they were supposed to be doing. Sometimes things got pretty nasty and architects would become defensive and strident about stopping the process. My theoretical basis of design is from the bottom up; and as I pointed out years ago, our architecture is the recipient of human energy. If it gets enough it pays you back with satisfaction. If you give it love and care and energy, it's good; and if it doesn't get enough and you've starved it, you don't get it back, it doesn't come alive and the whole thing just doesn't work. This seems to include everybody's energy: the users, the inhabitants, the bankers, the contractor, everybody – not just the architect. They need the architect's energy too, a good reason why the whole process of designing the building should be spread around to as many people as possible.

JS: It seems that before the Renaissance, people got involved. There wasn't an architect, there was architecture as a social art. After that, the idea of the architect as a hero solely responsible for work, to the exclusion of the client, became prominent. Basically, there are two parallels here. Traditional vernacular architecture and the community involvement are part of the same thing, aren't they? And this is what you're doing.

CWM: Sure, and I don't see why architects, contemporary architects, can't make something of that and enjoy vernacular strengths. They feel threatened by them or don't understand them, or they have been trained to think that they're terrible. I remember books when I was in high school by various architectural historians who contrasted the healthy Gothic with the pea-brained and sissified Renaissance; but that was for a very short time. I got caught up in that debate and saw both sides. I never really thought I was against a certain style of architectural design until I started teaching. There are several modern reversions – probably desperately to be mistrusted.

JS: Has architecture fallen into a fashion syndrome where we are doomed to go in cycles?

CWM: What we're going to do after Philip Johnson goes, I don't know. He invents these things one by one.

Opposite: *University of Washington Chemistry Department, Seattle*

SAN ANTONIO ART INSTITUTE
SAN ANTONIO, TEXAS

On a beautifully landscaped site in San Antonio a new 45,000 square-foot art college is sited to relate to an existing Spanish Colonial Museum and a small community art school. In order to create a sense of community and campus we organised the building around a series of courts and streets. A public pedestrian street is lined with a café, bookstore, gallery, auditorium and library. A more private street and court allow for student gathering, work and recreation. The two streets intersect at a large pavilion. This area serves as the main entrance to the school as well as a reception and celebration space for the auditorium, gallery, and café.

In the interest of economy and clear organisation, the budget for rich detailing is focused on entry areas and public rooms, while studios and classrooms are simple north-facing loft spaces. Many spaces are designed to accommodate multiple uses: the sculpture courtyard is terraced so that it can also serve as an informal amphi-theatre; the pavilion court can accommodate special parties and fund-raising activities; library reading rooms are shaped to double as special seminar rooms.

During the course of preliminary design, the entire board of the institute was involved in workshops to explore their goals and images for the new institution. These sessions were important in developing a unified commitment, that was later reflected in the successful fund-raising effort that exceeded its original seven million dollar goal.

Project: *San Antonio Art Institute;* Design Architect: *Moore Ruble Yudell;* Principal-in-charge, Principal Designer: *Buzz Yudell;* Principal Designer: *Charles Moore;* Principal Designer: *John Ruble;* Project Manager: *Renzo Zecchetto;* Project Manager, Schematic Design Phase: *Miguel Escobar;* Head of Production: *Alfeo B Diaz; Hong Chen, George Nakatani, Paul Nagashima, Steve Vitalich, James Mary O'Connor, Eric Mikiten*

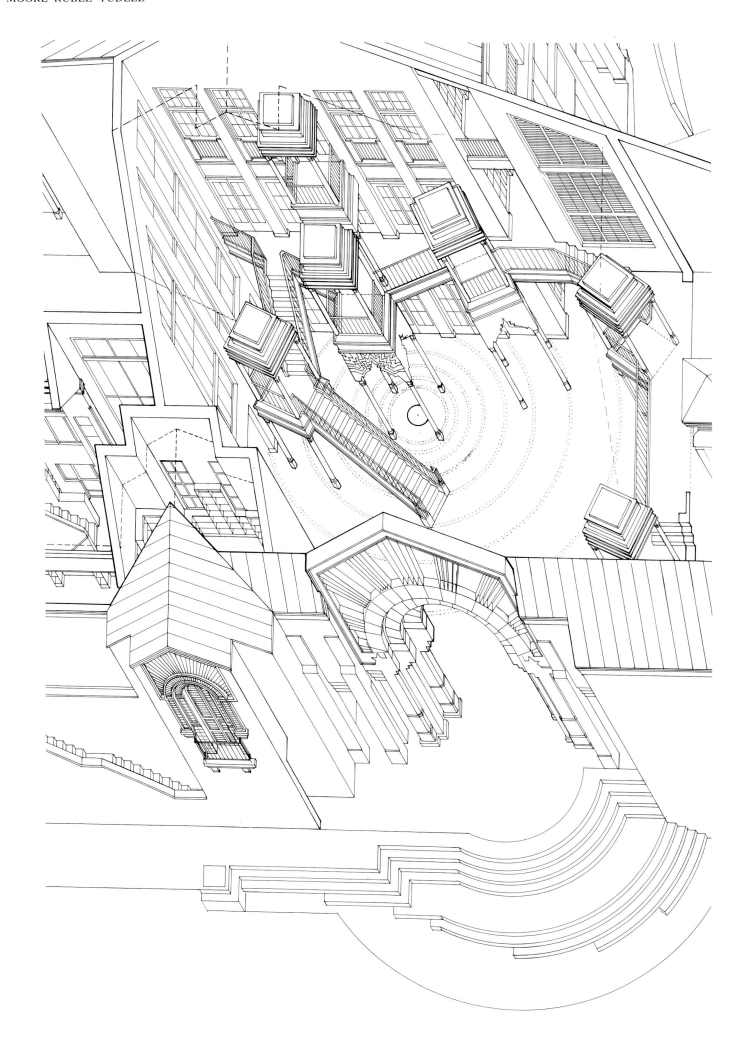

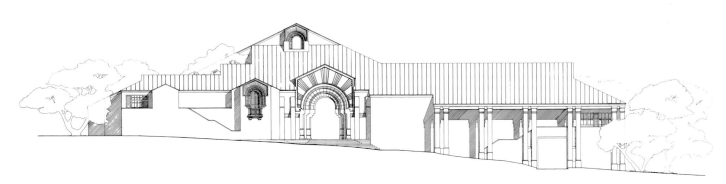

WEST ELEVATION

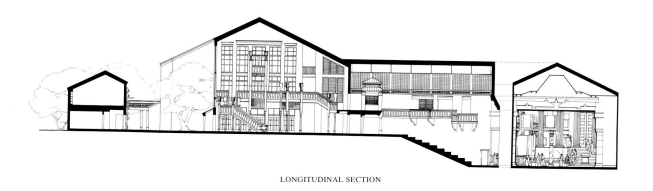

LONGITUDINAL SECTION

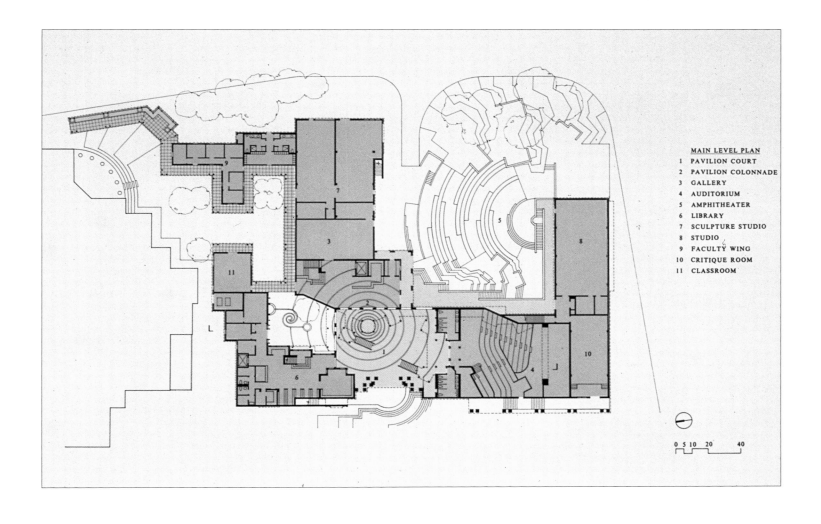

MAIN LEVEL PLAN
1 PAVILION COURT
2 PAVILION COLONNADE
3 GALLERY
4 AUDITORIUM
5 AMPHITHEATER
6 LIBRARY
7 SCULPTURE STUDIO
8 STUDIO
9 FACULTY WING
10 CRITIQUE ROOM
11 CLASSROOM

0 5 10 20   40

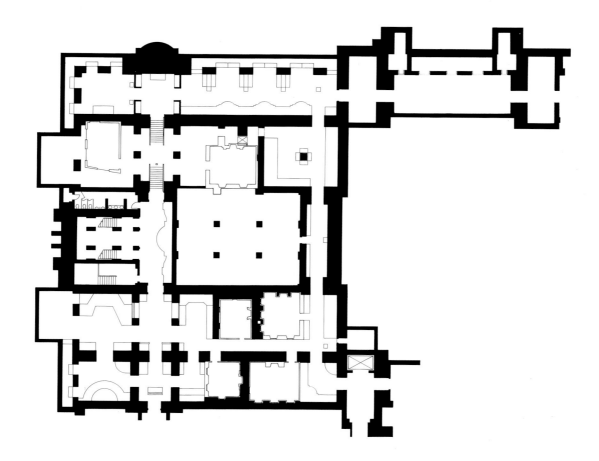

RENOVATIONS TO THE WEST WING
DECORATIVE ARTS GALLERIES, ST LOUIS ART MUSEUM
ST LOUIS, MISSOURI

In 1982, Moore Ruble Yudell was selected to renovate the West Wing galleries of the St Louis Art Museum. Our first task was to rethink a series of piecemeal alterations made to the building since the museum's introduction at the 1904 World's Fair, and to revive the intentions of Cass Gilbert, the building's celebrated first architect. Our goal has been to restore the museum to its original grandeur while providing state-of-the-art support systems for museum personnel.

This effort has included a variety of approaches. In the existing West Wing galleries, our replanning effort sought to restore the original 'plaid' of the plan, the Beaux-Arts order of cross-axes creating a matrix of linked rooms. The principal task was restorative, including the design of display cases and mouldings that reinterpret the ornate woodwork of the original galleries. An unused mechanical

shaft in the museum provided the opportunity to create a grand stair linking the restored West Wing galleries with the completely new decorative arts galleries in the basement level. The stair connects the new basement galleries to all levels. The new order created by the basement level recalls the Beaux-Arts plaid of the upper levels. Exhibition areas are organised by geography and period. Connections between objects of different places and times are encouraged through the use of axial views.

Project: *Renovations to the West Wing, Decorative Arts Galleries;* Owner: *St Louis Art Museum;* Design Architect: *Moore Ruble Yudell;* Principal-in-charge, Principal Designer: *Buzz Yudell;* Principal Designer: *Charles Moore;* Principal Designer: *John Ruble;* Project Manager: *Thomas Nagel; Doug Jamieson;* Associated Architect: *Smith-Entzeroth;* Colour: *Tina Beebe*

GROUND FLOOR PLAN

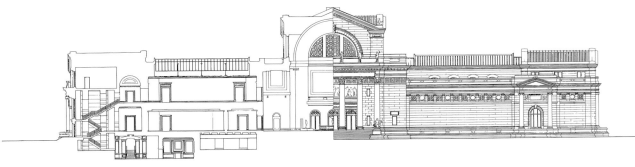

CENTRE: SECTION THROUGH WEST WING AND NORTH ELEVATION

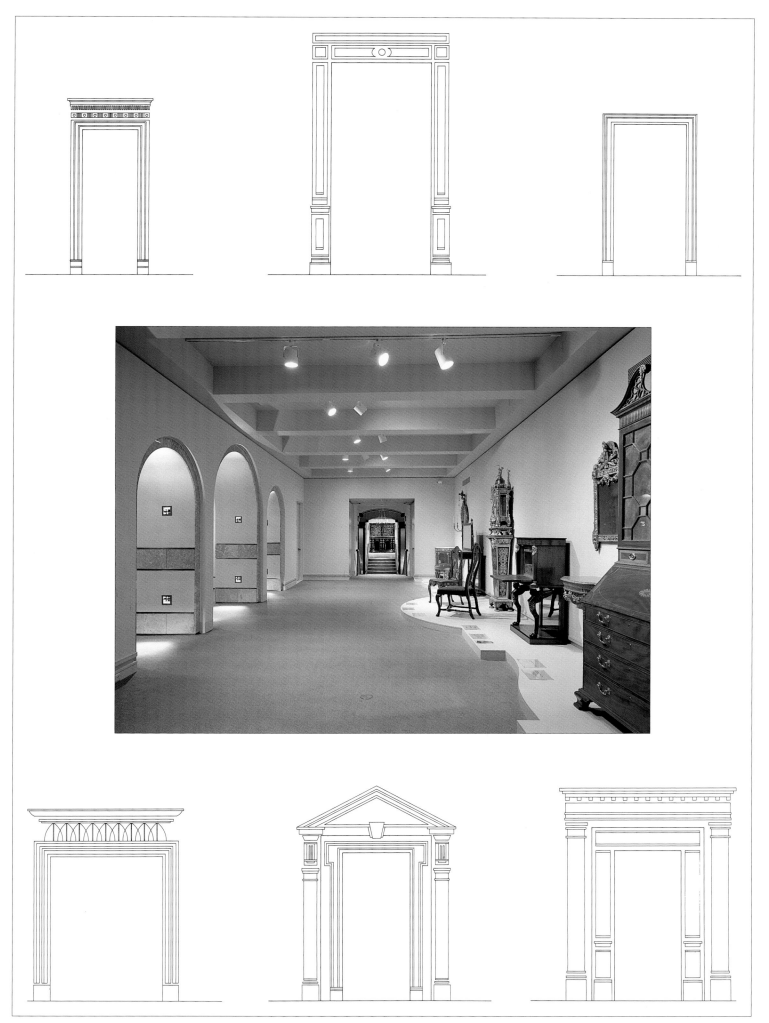

ABOVE AND BELOW: DOOR DETAILS

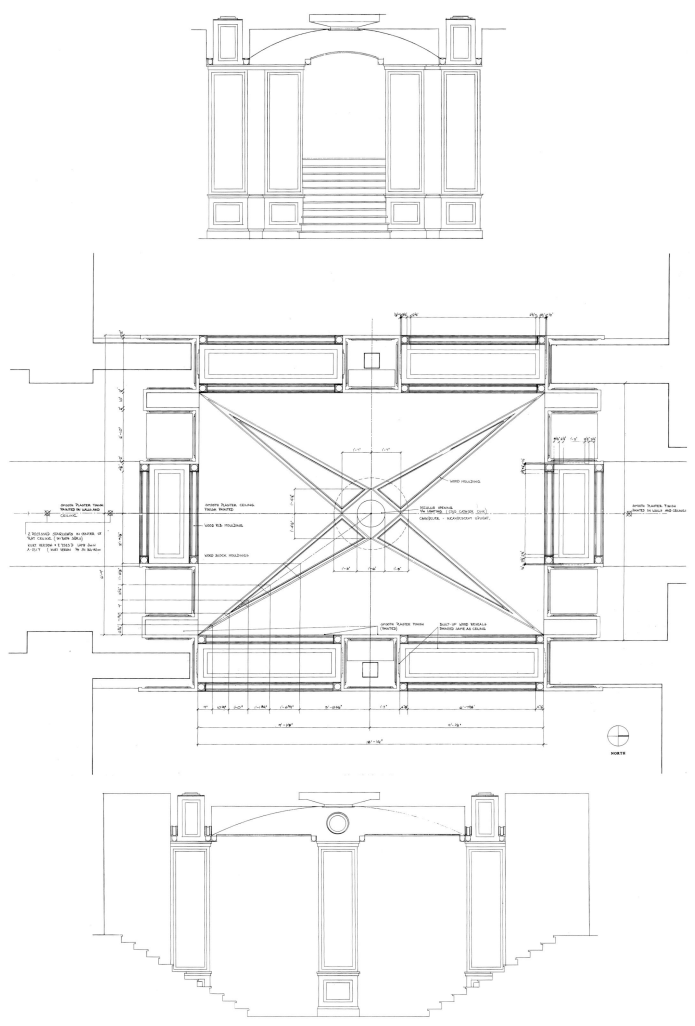

FROM ABOVE: TRANSVERSE SECTION OF STAIRCASE IN WEST WING; CEILING DETAIL; LONGITUDINAL SECTION OF STAIRCASE IN WEST WING

WALTER A HAAS SCHOOL OF BUSINESS
UNIVERSITY OF CALIFORNIA, BERKELEY

With a commanding site on an extraordinarily beautiful campus, the Walter A Haas School of Business – part of one of the world's foremost teaching and research universities – is a gateway to its own pleasant courts, plazas and rooms; from the community to the main campus, from the university to the business community, and from the West Coast to the growing commerce of the Pacific Rim. Designed to encourage interaction, the school is organised around a series of indoor and outdoor spaces that foster informal meetings and accommodate more formal gatherings as well.

The approach from the campus through a large gateway and across a courtyard culminates in the student 'forum'. This is the heart of the school: a large hall with a great cascade of steps that leads up through the various levels of the hillside site and doubles as seating and a place to overlook gatherings, lectures and performances. Student activity areas, classrooms and the faculty offices are located adjacent to the forum to ensure a critical mass of activity. The other major spaces of the Business School – a large lecture hall, the library's main reading room and a reception hall – surround the forum and reinforce its importance as a crossroads.

Rapidly changing technology and practice in business education required utmost flexibility in accommodating the school's varied activities. At the same time, the total amount of space required – over 200,000 square feet – presented a challenge: respecting the modest scale of *neighbouring buildings and the special character of the landscape. We divided the programme into three linked buildings: a classroom building, a building for offices and research, and a building for support activities including administration, library and computer centre. These are grouped to create a series of outdoor courts and plazas. From a formal entrance court on Gayley Avenue to a sloping glade that flows into adjacent Strawberry Creek, these outdoor places are shaped by buildings nestled into the hillside. Each has a distinctive character, and plays an important role for the school.*

Sloping roofs, thick walls of reinforced concrete and traditionally proportioned windows that contrast with glassy porches catching the winter sun; and bridges, gates, balconies and dormers give the business school a richness and vitality of form recalling the best architecture of the Berkeley campus and the Bay Area.

Project: *Walter A Haas School of Business;* Owner: *University of California, Berkeley;* Design Architect: *Moore Ruble Yudell;* Principal-in-charge, Principal Designer: *John Ruble;* Principal Designer: *Charles Moore;* Principal Designer: *Buzz Yudell;* Project Manager: *Stephen Harby; Christopher Kenney, Steve Gardner, Anton Vetterlein, Markku Kari, Angel Gabriel, James Mary O'Connor, Brian Tichenor, Mark Denton, John Taft, Arnold Swanborn, Ying-Chao Kuo;* Colour: *Tina Beebe;* Associate Architect: *VBN Corporation;* Landscape: *Arbegast, Newton and Griffith;* Lighting: *Peters & Myer*

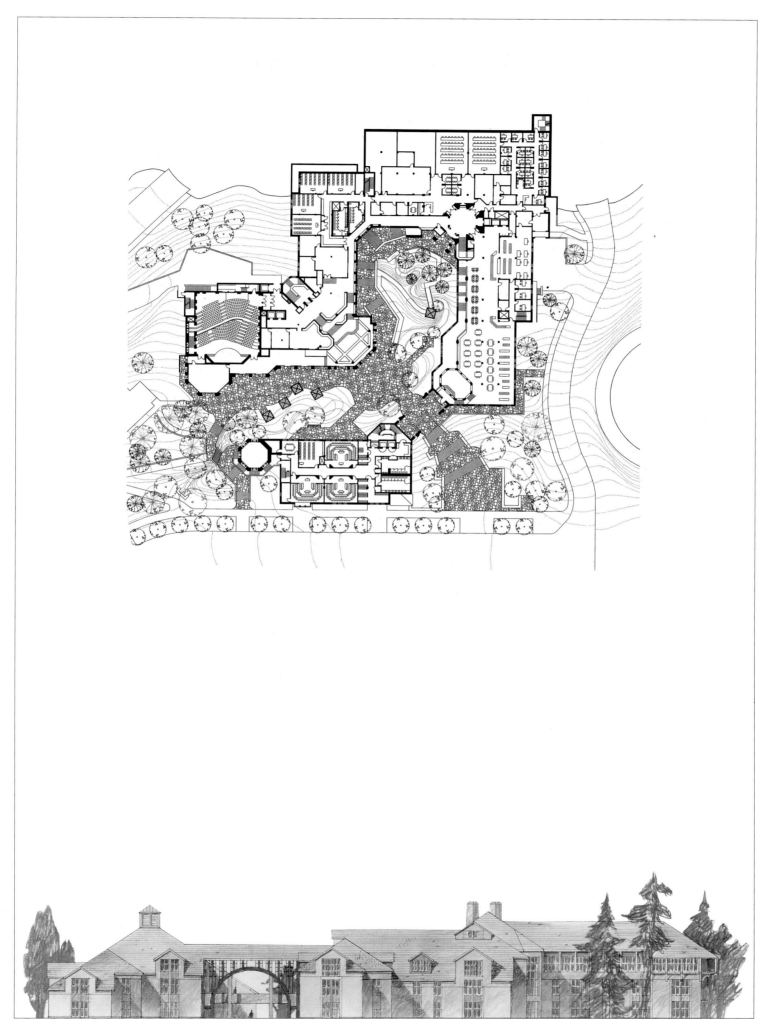

GROUND FLOOR PLAN AND FRONT ELEVATION

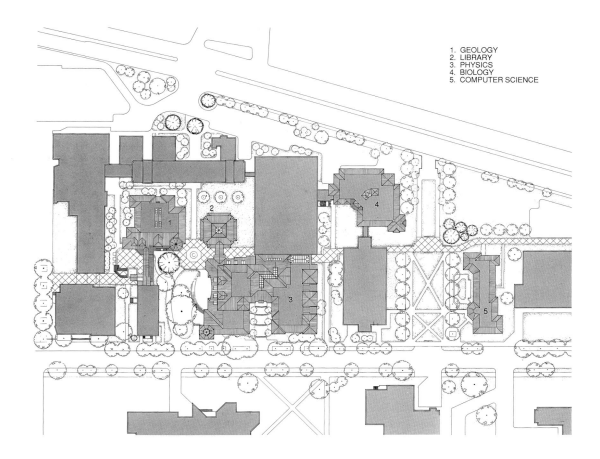

UNIVERSITY OF OREGON SCIENCE COMPLEX
EUGENE, OREGON

Moore Ruble Yudell was the design consultant for the University's new research laboratories and teaching spaces for the Biology, Physics, Geology, and Computer Science departments as well as expanded facilities for the Science Library. When we were retained for planning and design, two conditions seemed critical to the direction of our efforts. First, the original Beaux-Arts campus plan of 1914 had formed an elegant and successful armature for campus growth until the 1950s, but became abandoned as new buildings ignored streets, quadrangles and each other. Secondly, in the 70s Christopher Alexander had worked with the university planners to write The Oregon Experiment, *which called for user participation in the development of socially and physically sensitive patterns.*

We thus took as our challenge the restoration of the historic relation of buildings to streets and courts, hoping to use the new buildings to restore the original spatial and visual continuities of the campus; both on the scale of the campus plan and in the use of a palette of material: patterned brick, cast stone trim and copper roofs. Our planning and design process integrated aspects of Alexander's Oregon Experiment *with our own experience in participatory planning workshops. All major constituents of the campus were represented and helped shape the buildings at a departmental as well as site-planning level.*

The buildings function as discrete free-standing elements housing individual departments, organised vertically; and connect horizontally to form inter-disciplinary relationships critical to the way in which the sciences function. Bridges between departments house the offices of inter-disciplinary 'institutes'. More informal connection is made along a 'science walk' linking the buildings through a series of arcades and courts. Each building has

a series of important social spaces – from informal areas near clustered offices to departmental 'hearths' to courtyards. The heart of the project is a four-storey atrium bounded by classrooms, conference spaces, research laboratories and institutes. This and other major meeting areas are designed to maximise a south-facing orientation especially important in the north-west climate.

Laboratories, offices and social spaces evolved in close response to the particular nature of research and communication of each discipline. The scientists collaborated with us to model their specific research patterns and needs. A flat slab concrete structural system has been established to maximise flexibility and allow for appropriate bay modules for each department. Overhead mechanical services allow for quick changes in lab set-ups.

Design Architect: *Moore Ruble Yudell;* Principal-in-charge, Principal Designer: *Buzz Yudell;* Principal Designers: *Charles Moore, John Ruble;* Project Managers: *Stephen Harby, James B Morton; Hong Chen, Neal Matsuno, Bill Mochidome, William Murray, George Nakatani, James Mary O'Connor, Patrick Ousey, Richard Song, Renzo Zecchetto, Brian Tichenor, Katie Zobal;* Executive Architect: *The Ratcliff Architects;* Principal: *Christopher 'Kit' Ratcliff;* Project Director: *Christie Johnson Coffin;* Project Architect – Willamette and Deschutes Halls: *Carl Christiansen;* Streisinger Hall: *Stephannie Bartos;* Cascade Hall: *Tak Yamamoto;* Interiors Coordinator: *Yung Ling Chen;* Associated Architect: *Brockmeyer McDonnell;* Laboratory Consultant: *McLellan & Copenhagen;* Lighting: *Richard C Peters;* Landscape: *Royston, Hanamoto, Alley & Abey; Cameron & McCarthy;* Colour: *Tina Beebe;* Arts Administrator: *Lotte Streisinger;* Artists: *Kent Bloomer, Ed Carpenter, Wayne Chabre, Jane Marquis, Ken Von Roenn; Alice Wingwall; Scott Wylie*

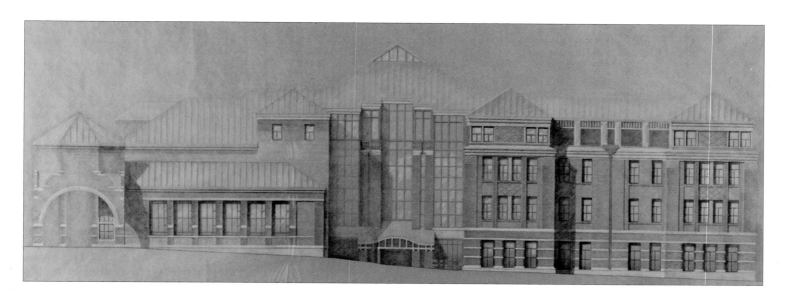

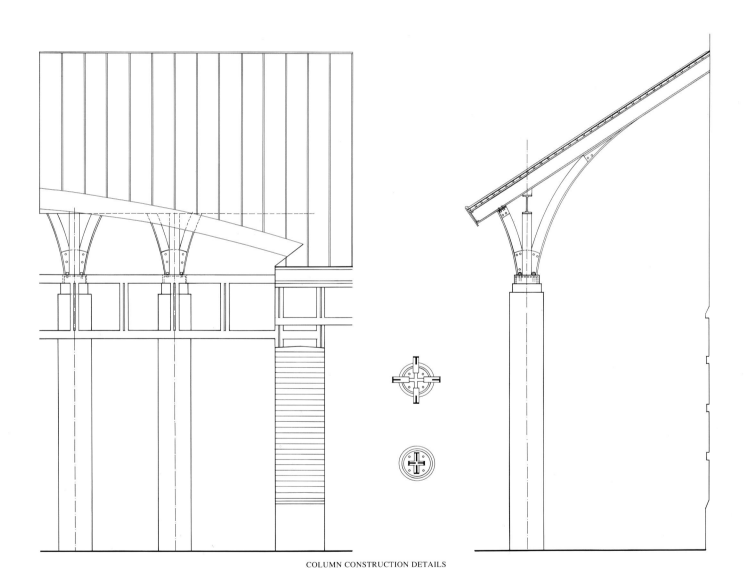

COLUMN CONSTRUCTION DETAILS

THE PETER BOXENBAUM ARTS EDUCATION CENTRE
CROSSROADS SCHOOL, SANTA MONICA, CALIFORNIA

*The Crossroads School, a lively and progressive second-
ary school, asked us to convert a simple, concrete warehouse building into a new facility for the visual and
performing arts. The campus is located in a dense, largely
industrial urban neighbourhood. We wanted to accept the
setting – the tough context of warehouse buildings – and
create a complementary tough elegance in the façade.
Cornice and base are established with precast concrete
and coloured plaster. A light monitor articulates the
building as it meets the sky, giving the building verticality
that strengthens its presence from the campus and beyond.*

*The campus is comprised of a row of former commer-
cial and warehouse structures fronting a public street,
with a common alley behind. The alley is the spine of the
campus – a private pedestrian street that serves as the hub
of campus gathering. The building needed an identity on
the street for public events as well as one on the alley.
These two entrances are connected by an internal plaza
and street that celebrate the daily interaction of the*
*students and the arts. Dance, art, and music studios have
windows and addresses along this internal street and
plaza. The second floor gallery can be opened onto the
plaza, allowing exhibitions the advantage of a larger
unified area; or it can be closed off for smaller shows and
security. The space is animated by a grand stairway,
punctuated with small landings that form eddies in the
flow of traffic. The stair and the plaza provide places for
events and performances: places to see and to be seen.
Since the opening of the Boxenbaum Centre, the plaza has
become the school's major celebration area.*

Project: *The Peter Boxenbaum Arts Education Centre, Cross-
roads School;* Owner: *Crossroads School;* Design Architect:
Moore Ruble Yudell; Principal-in-charge, Principal Designer:
Buzz Yudell; Principal Designer: *Charles Moore;* Principal
Designer: *John Ruble;* Project Manager: *Leon Glodt; Miguel
Escobar, Daniel Garness, Alfeo B Diaz, Hong Chen;* Lighting:
Richard C Peters; Colour: *Tina Beebe*

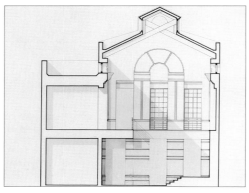

SECTION LOOKING WEST

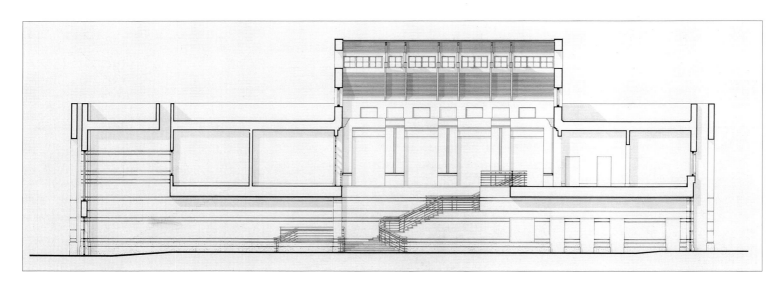

SECTION LOOKING NORTH; SECTION LOOKING SOUTH

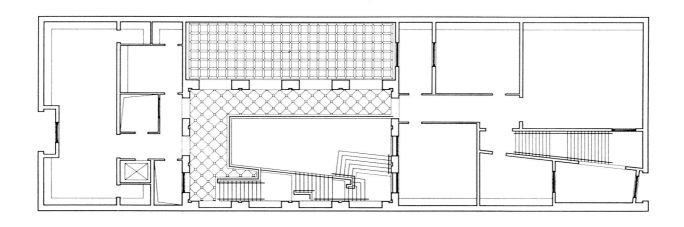

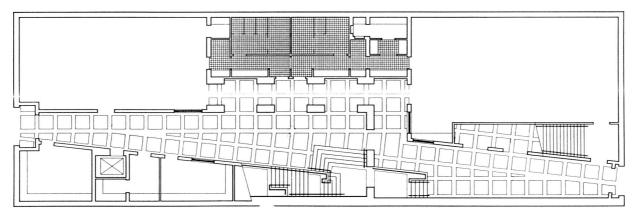

SECOND FLOOR PLAN; FIRST FLOOR PLAN

117

MOLECULAR BIOLOGY RESEARCH FACILITY UNIT II, III
UNIVERSITY OF CALIFORNIA, SAN DIEGO

This laboratory was financed through the occupancy agreement with a non-profit research institution. The owner and scientists wished the buildings to be as internally open as possible, with a variety of places for spontaneous meetings, which is at the very centre of their approach to science. Functionally, the labs are supported and connected by a central equipment corridor plus a spine of rooms for special use. Equally important were the qualities of natural light in the labs, a sense of the landscape, and distant views. The 678,000 square-foot building attaches to an existing Unit I via a bridge that also contains offices. In the basement, animal facilities and other equipment are shared by the two buildings. Relating carefully to Unit I, the much larger typical floor area of our building (18,000 square feet) is centred on an intimate court that is shaded grandly by a trellis and four colossal columns. This court, attended by a small 'tower' of conference rooms and animated by a grand stairway, is the social heart of the laboratory.

On the exterior, concrete block walls and towers anchor the long, open galleries of the laboratories. On the

west side, a grove of eucalyptus trees provides a shady background; and on the east side, a terraced lawn awaits a future Unit III to become a symmetrical courtyard.

Project: *Molecular Biology Research Facility, Unit II;* Owner: *Regents of the University of California;* Design Architect: *Moore Ruble Yudell;* Principal-in-charge, Principal Designer: *John Ruble;* Principal Designer: *Charles W Moore;* Principal Designer: *Buzz Yudell;* Project Managers: *Markku Kari, Michael de Villiers; James Mary O'Connor, Akai Ming-Kae Yang;* Associate Architect: *The Ratcliff Architects;* Laboratory Consultants: *Research Facilities Design;* Lighting: *Richard C Peters;* Artwork: *Jackie Ferrara;* Landscape: *The Spurlock Office;* Colour: *Tina Beebe*

Unit III (Phase 2): Design Architect: *Moore Ruble Yudell;* Principal-in-charge, Principal Designer: *John Ruble;* Principal Designer: *Charles W Moore;* Principal Designer: *Buzz Yudell;* Project Manager: *David Kaplan; Steve Gardner, Richard Destin, Christopher Kenney, Ying-Chao Kuo, John Taft, Craig Currie;* Associate Architect: *Lee, Burkhart, Liu*

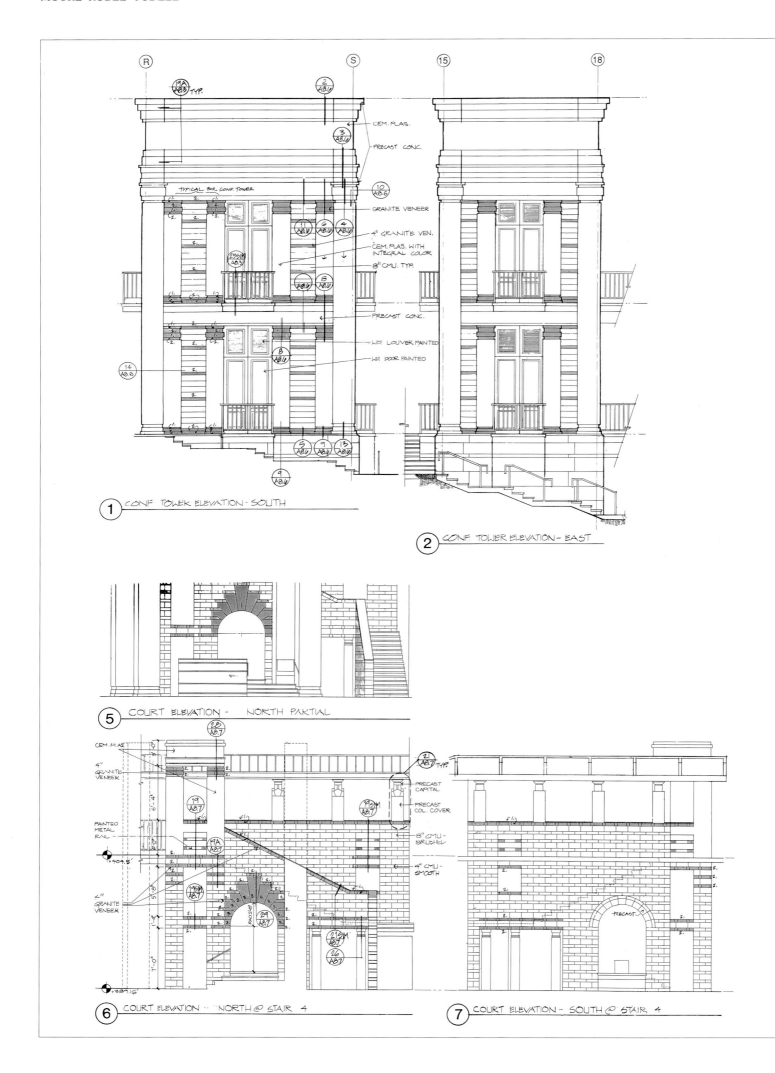

CEM. PLAS.

PRECAST CONC.

TYPICAL FOR CONF. TOWER

GRANITE VENEER

4" GRANITE VEN.

CEM. PLAS. WITH INTEGRAL COLOR

8" CMU. TYP.

PRECAST CONC.

WD. LOUVER PAINTED

WD. DOOR PAINTED

1 CONF. TOWER ELEVATION - SOUTH

2 CONF. TOWER ELEVATION - EAST

5 COURT ELEVATION - NORTH PARTIAL

CEM. PLAS.

4" GRANITE VENEER

PAINTED METAL RAIL

4" GRANITE VENEER

PRECAST CAPITAL

PRECAST COL. COVER

8" CMU - BRUSHED

4" CMU - SMOOTH

PRECAST

6 COURT ELEVATION - NORTH @ STAIR 4

7 COURT ELEVATION - SOUTH @ STAIR 4

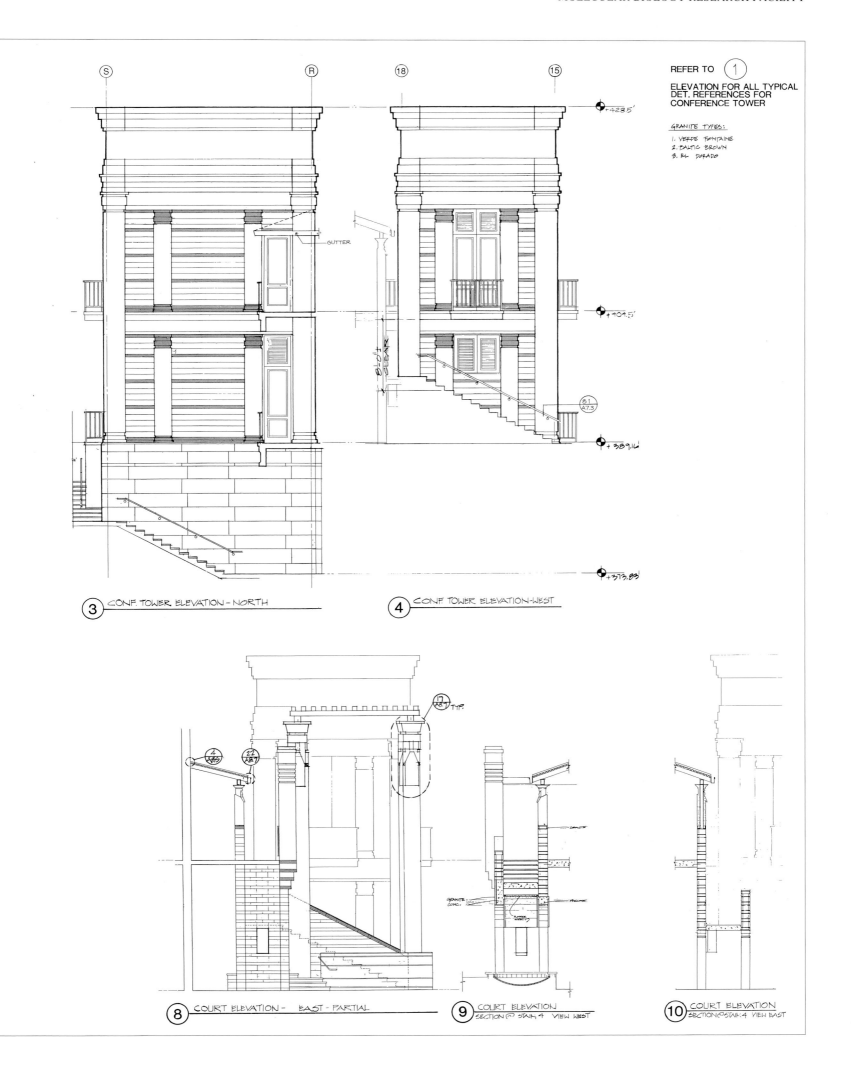

REFER TO ①

ELEVATION FOR ALL TYPICAL
DET. REFERENCES FOR
CONFERENCE TOWER

GRANITE TYPES:

1. VERDE FONTAINE
2. BALTIC BROWN
3. EL DORADO

③ CONF. TOWER ELEVATION – NORTH

④ CONF. TOWER ELEVATION – WEST

⑧ COURT ELEVATION – EAST – PARTIAL

⑨ COURT ELEVATION
SECTION @ STAIR 4 VIEW WEST

⑩ COURT ELEVATION
SECTION @ STAIR 4 VIEW EAST

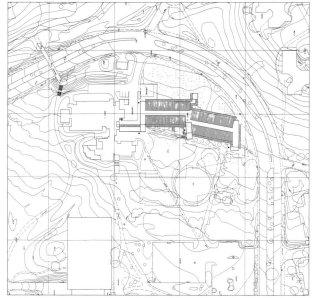

SITE PLAN

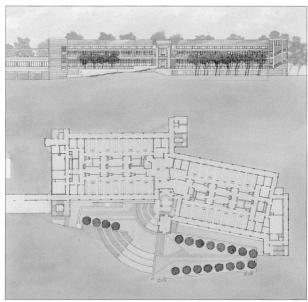

SOUTH ELEVATION AND GROUND FLOOR PLAN

THE CENTER FOR THE ARTS
ESCONDIDO, CALIFORNIA

The Center for the Arts in Escondido celebrates the arts and more: it creates a focus for a full range of civic habitation. It draws upon Southern California's architectural heritage in a fresh way, working with its site and context to create a cultural and civic heart for this rapidly growing community.

The Center for the Arts includes the Lyric Theatre, 1,532 seats; Community Theatre, 400 seats; Art Center; and the Conference Center. These four buildings are grouped to embrace Grape Day park and woven together with more than a dozen courtyards and gardens of varying size and scale. Each of these outdoor spaces has a distinct character and participates in a richly composed sequence to enrich arrival and movement through the Center.

The architectural expression of the Center for the Arts stemmed from respect for a recent accomplishment – the adjacent City Hall, and a long tradition – the distinctive architectural heritage of Southern California. A key aspect of this heritage is the play of quiet, understated moments against more active elements at critical points of entry and gathering; this selective concentration of architectural articulation offers visual punctuation and economical construction. Throughout the Center, elements such as towers, special windows and balconies, porches and arcades play against tranquil walls. This contrast of more simple and more rich forms heightens the impact of each, while landscape accentuates and enriches this rhythm. In addition, architectural elements are layered to integrate inside and outside – porches, arcades, pergolas and fountains draw the eye out across courts and plazas into the landscape.

While conceived as part of an interdependent whole, each of the Center's buildings responds to its particular requirements. The Art Center is a quiet, contemplative place of well-proportioned rooms and flexible north-facing studios enfronting a quiet garden. The Conference Center offers special meeting rooms, porches and a breezeway court to link its rooms to the outdoors. The Community Theatre is a carefully proportioned, intimate performance space for everything from school plays to chamber music. The Lyric Theatre combines the best elements of traditional theatre configuration with the latest technological advances in its house. Its lobby spills outdoors into the Lyric Court, to take advantage of Escondido's mild climate. With this generous 'outdoor room' at its heart, the Center for the Arts is a celebration of the extraordinary setting and spirit of the place.

Project: *The Center for the Arts;* Owner: *Community Development Commission, City of Escondido, California;* Design Architect: *Moore Ruble Yudell;* Principal-in-charge, Principal Designer: *Buzz Yudell;* Principal Designers: *Charles Moore, John Ruble;* Project Director: *James B Morton;* Design Co-ordinator: *Renzo Zecchetto;* Head of Production: *Alfeo B Diaz;* Project Manager, Lyric Theatre: *Martin Saavedra;* Project Manager, Community Theatre: *Hong Chen;* Project Manager, Conference Center: *Denise Haradem;* Project Manager, Visual Arts Center: *George Nakatani;* Project Manager, Site Development: *Neal Matsuno;* Project Team: *Linda Brettler, Camilo Carillo, Richard Destin, Ted Elayda, Angel Gabriel, Steve Gardner, John Johnson, Rebecca Kaplan, Shuji Kurokawa, Jesse Marcial, Cynthia Phakos, Geoffrey Siebens, Tony Tran, Eugene Treadwell, Duck Lee, Heather Trossman, George Venini;* Building Systems Consultant: *Ove Arup and Partners, California;* Theatre Consultant: *Theatre Projects Consultants;* Landscape Architects: *Burton and Spitz;* Colour: *Tina Beebe*

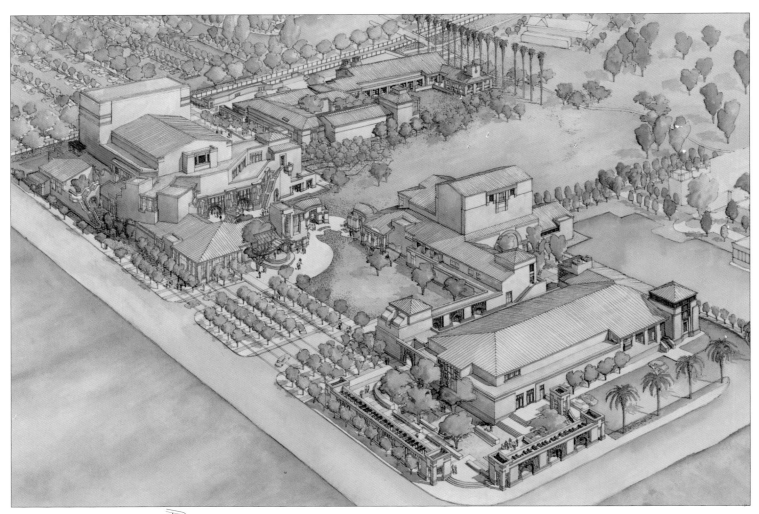

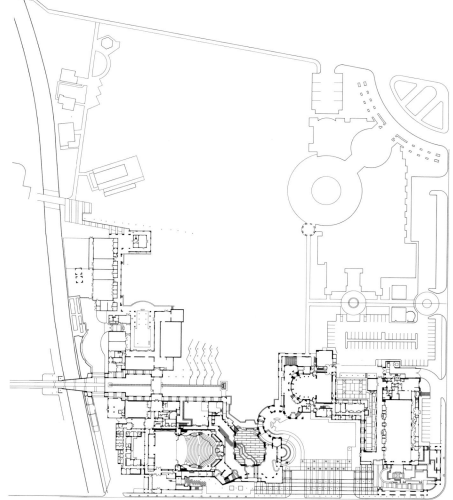

SITE PLAN

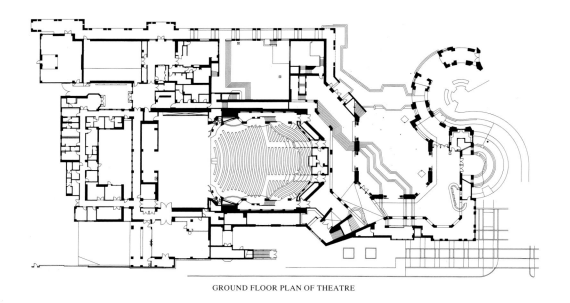

GROUND FLOOR PLAN OF THEATRE

UNIVERSITY OF WASHINGTON CHEMISTRY BUILDING
SEATTLE, WASHINGTON

The first project to receive construction funding as part of a major new building programme, the University of Washington Chemistry Building embodies the University's renewed commitment to science instruction – which includes providing first-class research facilities to attract top faculty, and at the same time sets the architectural tone for new campus development in the 1990s.

Sited at the heart of the campus, adjacent to Rainier Vista – a grand axial series of open spaces oriented to a distant view of Mt Rainier – the new building must work with a varied set of neighbours. It will connect directly to the existing Chemistry Building, Bagley Hall, the campus' only example of 1930s Art Deco architecture, and will relate to a series of older brick 'campus gothic' buildings surrounding a major campus plaza and fountain. It must also fit carefully into the site's extraordinary landscape, which includes a nearby important grove of trees defining an edge of Rainier Vista, and a beloved medicinal herb garden, one of the nation's oldest still in existence.

As with all our projects, the first step has been to listen: to encourage client and user involvement in the design process from its earliest stages – which in this case

included a series of four participatory design workshops that have formed the core of our programming effort. Workshop sessions have considered issues as broad as overall campus planning and as detailed as the length of a bench for a typical organic research work-station. In each workshop, faculty, students, staff and other interested members of the university community have worked in small groups to delve into the issues and propose approaches and answers.

The large and enthusiastic response to this participatory design process has already resulted in thoughtful, informative and creative contributions to the project that will be invaluable in subsequent phases of design.

Project: *Chemistry Building;* Owner: *University of Washington;* Design Architect: *Moore Ruble Yudell;* Principal-in-charge, Principal Designer: *John Ruble;* Principal Designer: *Charles W Moore;* Principal Designer: *Buzz Yudell;* Project Manager: *Stephen Harby; Christopher Kenney, Sylvia Deily, Wendy Kohn, Mark Denton, Yvonne Yao, Julie Malork, Ying-Chao Kuo;* Colour: *Tina Beebe;* Associated Architects: *Loschky, Marquardt & Nesholm;* Landscape Architect: *Murase Associates*

CHEMISTRY DEPARTMENT

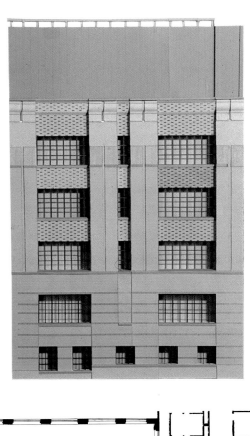

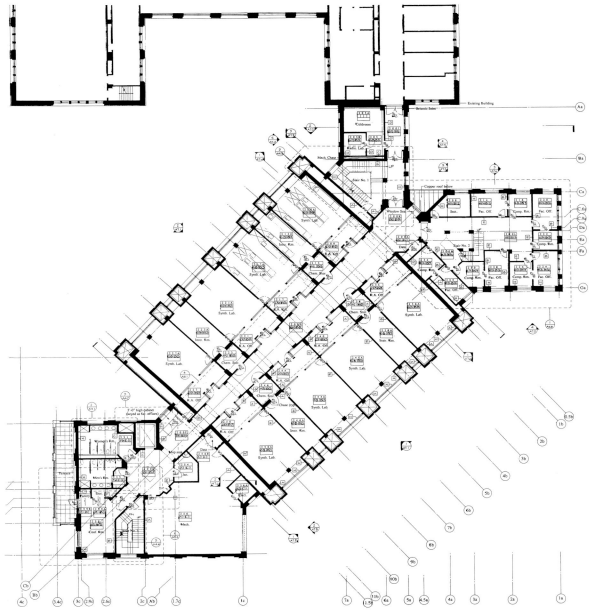

PLAN OF EXTENSION

CAROUSEL PARK
SANTA MONICA, CALIFORNIA

The Santa Monica Pier, with its historic Carousel, is one of the city's most endearing attractions. Carousel Park, the first in a series of major improvements, provides a new entry from Ocean Front Walk, giving equal access to the south side of the Pier where a new commercial promenade is envisioned.

Facing Ocean Park Promenade, the entry plaza is at once a gateway to the Pier, a meeting point for pedestrians and an open theatre for strollers, bicyclists, skateboarders, rollerskaters, and other performers. Its octagonal shape is derived from the shape of the Carousel towers, and its ramps and steps celebrate the connection of the pier to the land, reinforcing the sense of leaving the land and going 'on board' the Pier.

The pier deck surrounding the carousel has been extended approximately fifty feet east, to allow for seating and viewing on top and increased retail space along the promenade below. Its exterior elevation complements the façade of the carousel building above.

A children's park of approximately 5,000 square feet is located at the southern edge of the site. Its planting of palms, Australian tea trees and turf suggests a miniature of historic Palisades Park on the bluffs above. A dragon of river-washed granite boulders slithers through the park, becoming steps at the lowest end, an amphitheatre retaining wall and bench at the top. The dragon glares with amber-lit eyes at a boat riding upon his back, while his flaring nostrils hiss with a watery mist.

Just around the corner from the children's park, the pier deck steps down in amphitheatre seating along the volleyball courts. Two observation pavilions provide an overlook and with their festive bright lights anticipate the future development of the south side of the Pier.

Project: *Carousel Park, Santa Monica Pier;* Owner: *City of Santa Monica;* Design Architect: *Moore Ruble Yudell with Campbell and Campbell (joint venture);* Principal-in-charge, Principal Designer: *John Ruble;* Project Designer: *Buzz Yudell;* Project Manager: *Peter Zingg; James Mary O'Connor, Stephen Vitalich, Dan Garness;* Structural Engineers: *Gordon Polon;* Mechanical Engineers: *Howard Helfman and Associates;* Landscape Architects: *Campbell and Campbell*

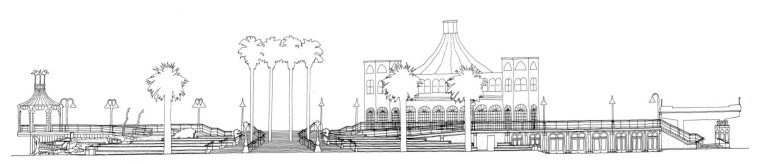

ABOVE AND BELOW: SOUTH ELEVATION; EAST ELEVATION

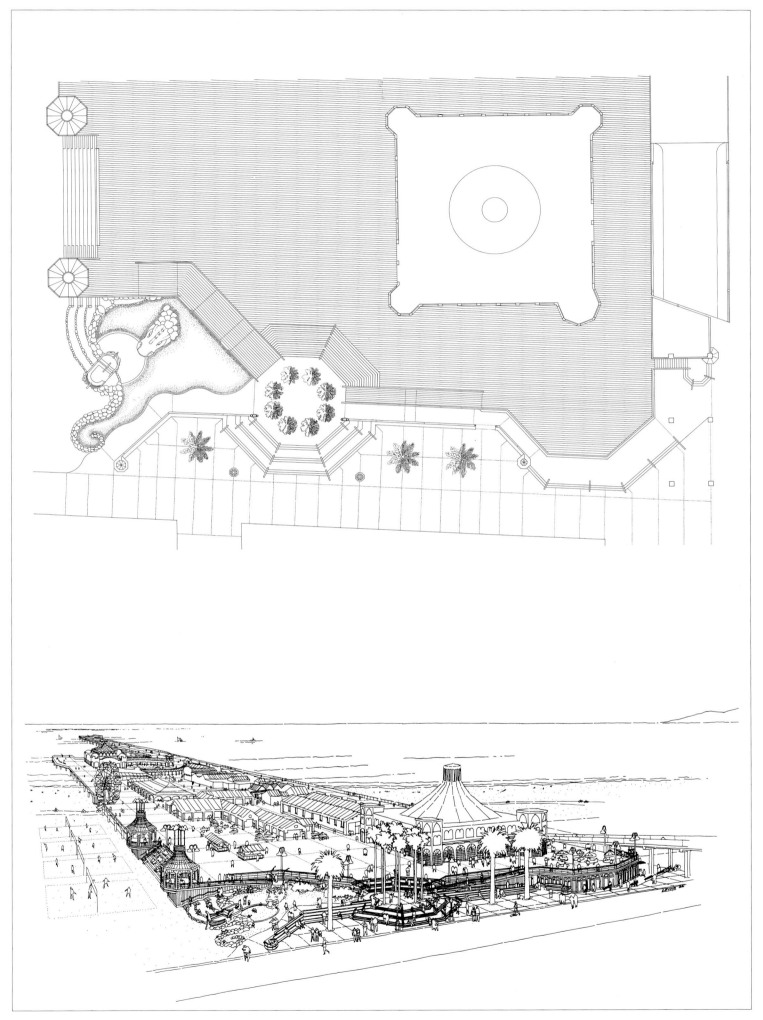

FROM ABOVE: GROUND FLOOR PLAN; PERSPECTIVE

THE FIELDTRIP
JOHN RUBLE

The Castle at Hell's Rock

Dear Buzz and Charles, It turns out that we started our trip here, fjord-hopping from Bergen almost to the Arctic Circle. We then spent two days of cross-country skiing and packing, before we finally stood at this lonely outpost in the Jule terminal moraine. Miraculously, Klaus is still here with his wife, working away on his selfless mission. I was a child when we last saw him, but he was, of course, completely unchanged: the portly good cheer, rosy complexion, white hair and beard still skirting a polished dome that almost rivals yours, Charles.

Their home, which Klaus laughingly refers to as Hell's Rock, was a hastily-built redoubt defended by the Knights of Inverness during a ninth-century invasion of Norway. Norsemen later took the castle, and over time added their own finishing touches – savage Celtic carving covers every wood surface in the great hall, and the fireplace sports the horns of every horned beast, save the reindeer. Klaus has carefully restored the scribblings of ancient sagas which line the walls of most rooms, and he's even provided translations into four languages! C was nervous at first about the little people but soon set to

work testing her theories on Nordic pre-Christian geometry. Needless to say, Klaus was overbearingly proud of his latest invention – the homing beacon for his sturdy Sikorsky, which he calls his 'cyber-sleigh'. Just downhill from the castle, the beacon makes an uncanny sight in a landscape that is little changed in the last thousand years. Klaus would have explained in endless detail how the beacon draws power from electrostatic charges in the night sky, but we were too distracted by the prospect of exploring caverns full of ancient weapons, suits of armour, and toy soldiers as big as life.

The Königssessel

This little-known chunk of rock in the Baltic has been claimed at different times by all the Hanseatic peoples, although eventually the German name stuck. Nothing was built here until the end of the seventeenth century when the powerful Bishop of Danzig commissioned plans for a nunnery by the Bavarian monk Nicolas of Weingarten, who was thought to have later assisted Balthazar Neumann. The buildings are modestly realised by baroque standards, with one notable exception – the mere fact of building on this tiny outcrop must be seen as wildly extravagant! What may have been 'Batissomanie' to the environmentalists of the day, is pure delight to us now. You arrive by boat at a small landing on the north side, and climb a gentle stair past a great vaulted wine-cellar, arriving at the Rettungsplatz just at the foot of the clock tower. The Sisters are vague about how the Rettungsplatz got its name: saving souls? Desperate seaman seeking refuge from the storm? The impression is that you'd be

blown away in a storm if you found yourself anywhere on this immense flat terrace, which seems to be laid out as a UFO landing site. Apparently, the top of the rocky island – barely three hundred metres in diameter – was levelled at some time prior to the seventeenth century, and rough boulder retaining walls were raised against the sea; but by whom, and for what reason? The Sisters are particularly unhelpful about such questions, and the oldest manuscripts in the library have all to do with horticulture and zoology. All very well, but none of this prepares you for the chapel interior: a series of nine great stone arches supporting the gable roof. Between each arch, vaults of carved and painted plaster depict the story of the creation on one side and the four Gospels of the New Testament on the other – all allegorically, using animal characters! Christ is, of course, a man, and Mary a woman, with the eagle, ox, man, and lion of the apostles. But around them a supporting cast of reptiles, mammals, birds and insects plays out each story in a garden whose wild transformations of morphology and colour would have astonished Goethe. It's as if someone tried to weave the sum total of scientific knowledge into the Bible – the philosophical foundation of the time – creating a complete panorama of human and divine thought. Dozens of tiny roof windows ingeniously seem to light the entire ceiling from within. Should you wish to see the chapel, letters must be written months ahead, and it helps to mention Dimitri.

Die Befreiung

While stopping in Berlin, we couldn't resist an evening at the new Meta-Theater, a tiny venue in the former Hannes Dieckman Strasse on the east side. 'Die Befreiung' – the Variance – deals with an everyday nightmare in Kafkaesque extremes: a simple, honest builder struggles with the German building codes while trying to remodel a small waterfront garage into a home and work place. C was bored with the text, finding it too much like Kafka, but I was totally spellbound; for, from scene to scene the set was transformed to represent the increasingly bizarre agreements, compromises and back-alley deals being made. Here was architecture reflecting the tangled webs of our social contract! Finally, after losing his wife to the building inspector, his money to the east-side mafia, and his soul to an

obscure 'expediter' named Getz, the builder gives a third act soliloquy that is at once heart-rending and hilarious. He stands on a little balcony, which was his only victory (and of course 'all he wanted' was to have a little balcony from which to watch the river as boats of drunken pals float by on Father's Day) and tries to convince us that it was worth it, that at least no one can take this balcony away from him because here in his pocket is 'meine Befreiung'. As the curtain falls, Getz peeks out from the little doorway, looking as if unfinished business is at

hand. Afterwards, we met the usual crowd at Transform-Keller and stayed for breakfast.

Murzynkiem Station

Buzz, I'm so glad you urged us to arc through eastern Europe on our way south; otherwise we would never have discovered Sgridz – and who could have imagined that a town so small would have a subway! It was built by the Russian army for Stalin's first post-war tour, and they had the good taste to rebuild the churches as stations. Here is the jewel of them all – Saint Gregory's on Murzynkiem Square. Could any city claim a more splendid terminus for its underground rails? The entry front and vaulted ceilings are entirely ceramic, glazed in soft rose and white, with random dots of cobalt and persimmon red. Tina would really love it, except that inside the icons have all been removed and replaced with the most outrageous radiant gas heating elements. Imagine a spiralling cone of black mesh projecting some four feet from the wall with a polished steel orb at its apex. From inside the cone a gas flame blasts out to heat the mesh and create radiation. If that weren't strange enough, the local utilities seem to supply natural gas in bursts, so that

From above: Die Befreiung; Murzynkiem Station

all of the radiant cones – there were dozens – coughed rhythmically into flames at precisely the same time, after which there was an audible sigh of relief from the frozen crowd moving through the

station: hffmpf...hahhh...hffmpf... hahhh...hffmpf! This performance was almost as arresting as the play of fading winter light across the hand-painted tile murals of biblical landscapes.

Somewhere near Gorizia

As we flew over the border between Slovenia and Northern Italy, we couldn't believe the sight this town presented below; nor could we find anything like it on the map. After arriving in Venice, we took a car north and searched for a week without success! All I have to show for it is this hasty little sketch from the window of the Airbus. Unless I am mistaken, the entire village is dug into a flat silty plain, covered uniformly with grasses still dry and golden-brown from the winter. Was this Italo Calvino's theme park, or what . . .? It almost certainly lies on the border, with its left side in Italy and its right side in Slovenia. Suddenly it occurred to C that the village was not actually lived in, but was the site of some pageant or festival, since it consisted almost entirely of streets, squares and one or two public buildings. Then we began to wonder – what happens in new housing projects all over Europe? Do they have festivals at all? Is someone busy creating new festivals that don't need streets and squares? Does it all happen on television instead? Perhaps a movement was now at work that was furiously digging

these hidden townscapes across the continent, irrespective of borders and languages, to be ready for the day when millions of inhabitants would storm out of the apartment blocks, looking around for some place to celebrate, say, the coming of summer.

Port Livja

This once breathtaking little harbour now merely reminds us that ever since the Fertile Crescent, cities have been the natural theatres of war. And what fragile artifacts they are – hundreds of years in the making, and levelled in days; the flattened, blackened evidence that our vanity lies in our causes, not in our works! We bent over the ruins, in the midst of wildest grief, to study them carefully, and hoped that our presence signalled the return of some kind of

daily life, like the café tables that had slowly begun to reappear. We had wanted to send you dazzling views of colourful merchants' houses, marching like a string-band parade into the market place. All we have is this plan which, come to think of it, suggests a waterfront town toughened by countless battles. Livja had its share of cannonades and cleverly concealed hiding places dug into the hillside. We were fascinated to see this arrangement confirmed as we aided Dimitri's uncle during several days of

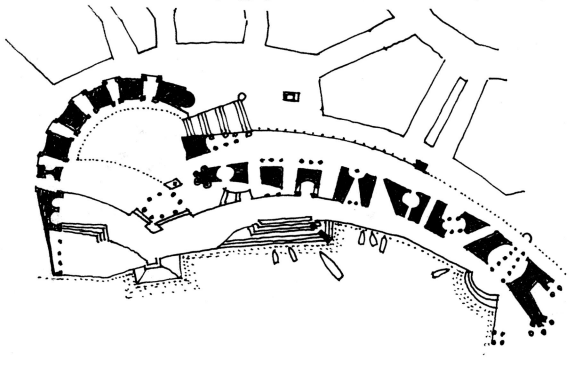

From above: *Somewhere near Gorizia; Il Tambore; Port Livja*

back-breaking labour in clearing the opening to his warehouse cavern behind the market. Exhausted, we sat as if in a dream, taking tea amid his well-protected treasures: the contraband animal hides, endangered reptiles, Roman amphora still filled with wine, and row upon row of silver putti cavorting wildly, and lovingly polished by the servants twice a day, for they do not hold their shine in the salt air.

Il Tambore

Renzo had some remarkable stories about Pastalleria, but even he didn't know about this villa – locally known as Il Tambore. We might hardly have mentioned it, though it is one of the two oldest houses on the island, but for an extraordinary geological feature: it happens to be built over one of the biggest limestone domes in the Mediterranean. Moreover, the rock beneath the central courtyard is in some places only two feet thick, and below that a huge domed cavern, some two hundred feet high, vaults over a rocky salt-water pool at the bottom. (Yes, there are blind shrimp, served only once a year in red jackets of hot Tunisian chilli pods.) Of course, now it's forbidden to even walk across the courtyard and everyone tip-toes around the edge. But legend has it that horses clattering their hooves on the stone pavement, as directed by their trainers, kicked up a booming drumbeat that was heard as far away as Cap Bon! You can enter the dome cavern by an old chain hanging just inside the little aperture on the stairway. It's a great place to store wine! Pastallerians are to this day resentful that the Romans never revised the *Aeneid* to include a stop here.

Hamam Aïn Sakhar

You can see the profile of the Hamam for several days as you make your way across the expanses of Oued Kebir, south from Tatahouine, and already you know something is amiss. So oddly recumbent, like a wounded bedouin knight waiting for the vultures, the gesture is also defiant, lacking the Islamic acceptance of fate. You will therefore not be surprised to learn that the construction is pre-Islamic, even pre-Roman, and reworked down the centuries by succeeding tribes. In Sousse we had met Ives, who wanted to investigate the ruins as a site for the French Touring Clubs, and we accepted his invitation to come along. We could hardly have expected what and whom we found there when we arrived: a tiny café and four or five guest rooms operated by – get this – a young Algerian with a degree from the Statler at Cornell! And he knows Don! After a long round of cocktails and tall tales we took rooms and changed, ready to begin exploring. The Hamam has three principal water sources, all at slightly different temperatures, with a structure built over each. Although the spaces are dimly lit, they are best experienced without torches; the shadowy carvings and richly painted walls and vaults form a dense collage of eternal truths and sudden vulgarities, like a vast graphic novel, begun in

Egyptian times, and continuously re-written. Even now it seemed to be changing, to keep our attention, and from noticing something else that may have happened here just hours ago: look, fresh paint! Our favourite room was beneath the pyramidal temple on the left: a hypostyle hall of tall piers supporting stone vaults, with a network of delicately ornamented balconies, bridges, stairs and shuttered rooms like tree houses, set among the piers at various heights. Presumably, the bathers moved from the open hall up to these private *cabinets* for massage, meditation,

or assignations of a more intimate nature. The baths must have been a great place to do business, as criss-crossing caravans met, bringing treasures and news from all the far-flung world. Why then was Aïn Sakhar so long deserted? We began to suspect the water. Mineral deposits around the pools soon confirmed the unusual name – sugar spa – for they were not salty, but astonishingly sweet!

I stared dumbly into the dark steamy pool, as if it held an answer, then gasped at the disappearing sight of a hollow face in the water. Ben-Bellah, our young host, found my story mildly amusing and sat us down to *briks à l'oeuf* and a *tajine à la tête d'agneau* that surpassed our wildest adventures.

La Maison de l'harmonie familiale

After a few days in Fez, we met Monghia Emerson, a young Moroccan *architecte diplômée* who had studied at the AA. We hired a car to visit one of her projects in a small town in the Atlas Mountains. Monghia had recently restored an unusual shrine that was devoted not to the typical *marahbouts*, but to family life. The house had been built in a breach in the town wall in the mid-1600s. For centuries it was the home of the descendants of Hassan Al-Sayyid Akhbar, famous for his poems of devotion to his wife. The house is, indeed, a splendid example of the regional idiom, as it spreads through a series of

From above: *Ruins at Hamam Aïn Sakhar; The House of Marital Harmony*

courtyards, beautiful salons and roof gardens, all framed by battered walls studded with bays of dense Moroccan lattice. But it was Al-Sayyid's wife, Melika, who provided Monghia with such a deep sense of connection to the project. She was in fact an architect and had designed the most captivating feature of the house: a pair of towers, which seem to break boldly through the rough stone palisade. Between the towers a dense and altogether picturesque garden comes as a complete shock once you

understand that it was carefully planned. Melika created the upper tower for her husband, as a kind of poet's retreat. The lower tower stands completely free, reached by a covered bridge across the plunging terraces. It was here that the family enjoyed their ritual morning meals and that the women of succeeding generations drew strength from Melika's vaults and domes of saturated primary colour – another stunningly 'modern' treatment.

El Parador del Caballo Azul

Another friend of Dimitri's (you know him from the trip to San Cristobal) is now running this little inn and equestrian school, El Parador del Caballo Azul, about an hour's drive from Lerida. A bell in the tower can be heard miles away on the trails which take you variously past olive groves to the rocky hilltop at Puroy. Here, a little village in total ruin awaits, for picnics or the occasional overnight. Apparently, there really was a blue horse, who was so revered that he lived not in the stables, but in the house. His master, Father Francesc de Roques, would often tie the animal to the lower porch so that travellers would stop in wonder while crossing the little bridge. Unfortunately, a local girl in despair at the beast's unaccountable beauty threw herself into the river, somewhat romantically, and was never found. Father Francesc, fearing reprisal, took the animal to Saragossa and sold him to a Dutchman.

La Sangrienta Casa Dorada

Renzo put us on to this one too, and it took over a week of vertigo-inspired rail travel to reach. But what a miraculous, impossible collision of place and culture! Sir Leslie Ellis-Burroughs, a Welsh surveyor and heir to a mining fortune, who may have been a distant relative of Sir Clough W-E, came to this Peruvian plateau in the 1820s. Using local masons and teaching them to make plaster, he raised this chunky, nougat-white, gothic hacienda during the next forty years. He then lovingly and heavily ornamented every crenellation and crocket in gold from a nearby vein he discovered. After the death of his first wife, the little chapel at the left became the scene of increasingly grim sacraments, better left undisclosed. Poor Sir Leslie's last years of his life were spent chained to his bed in darkest madness while Concepcion, his second wife, directed her brood of oddly blue-eyed children to strip away the gold ornaments on the house. The chapel, however, was left undisturbed. It would have been Sir Leslie's mausoleum had all the men in the region not been terrified to enter. It seems so harmless now, gleaming through gaps in the morning mist. However, its allure is deceptive: the lovely white and gold exterior conceals inner chambers of midnight red.

The Rosemont Artists' Building

No sooner had we returned than we were reminded that you never know what will happen next in this town. Leo asked us to dinner with a young Viennese architect who has just remodelled the old Rosemont Hotel into luxury condominiums and art studios – for women only! As you may recall, this splendid old tower from the 20s was really scrambled in the last earthquake: stairways went to different floors, some rooms abruptly became two-storey lofts, and French balconies suddenly imploded to become real loggias. On the top floor the water tower collapsed into an old boiler room, creating a heated pool. It was simply too exciting to continue as a cut-rate residential hotel. Clearly, this young architect has been influenced by your fantasy sketches, Charles; but with the seismic touch, the façades also look like high-rise land art. I think she's done a marvellous job, creating a sparkling image of collective life in a crumbling society. I guess the Viennese could teach us a thing or two about that! I look forward to seeing you both in a few days. Cheers, John.

From above: El Parador del Caballo Azul; La Sangrienta Casa Dorada

149

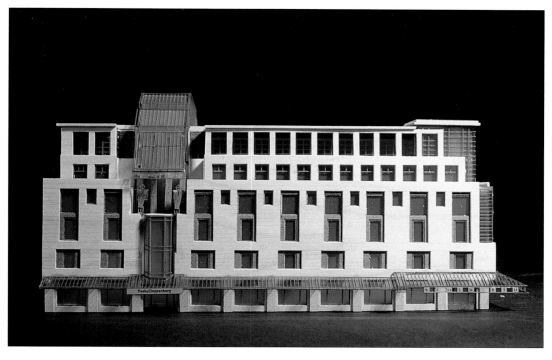

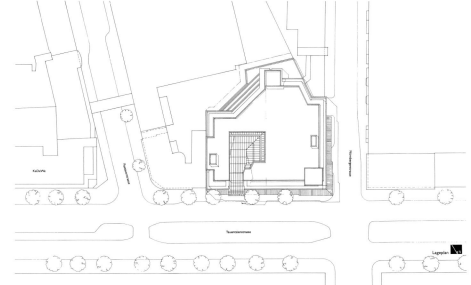

CENTRE: SITE PLAN

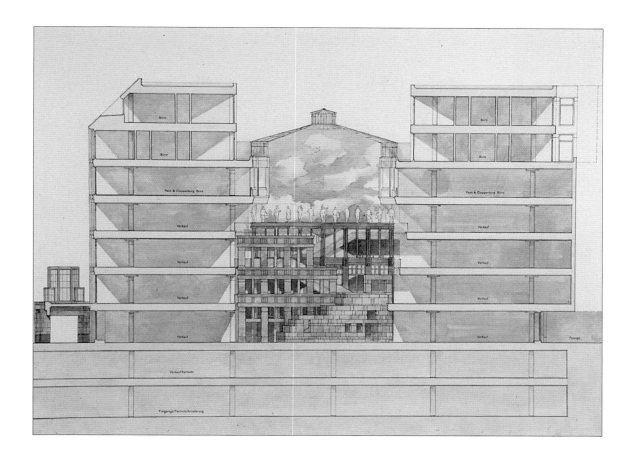

PEEK & CLOPPENBURG
LEIPZIG, GERMANY

The German department store chain Peek & Cloppenburg asked us for a proposal for their first department store in Leipzig, to be located in the historic city centre. The challenges of the site included the need to tie the new department store into a network of passages which are a distinctive feature of the city, and for the façade to mediate between narrow medieval street fronts and those of wider post-war set-backs. The building includes 17,500 square metres on seven floors – four floors of retail sales area and three floors of offices, with the flexibility to convert one office floor into a sales floor in the future.

As with our project for Berlin, the intention is to make

the experience of moving through the store a dramatic, almost theatrical one. Escalators and stairs between large interior façades facing a generous multi-level atrium, draw shoppers up through stage-like sets, with the atrium providing a point of orientation throughout the store.

Project: *Peek & Cloppenburg, Leipzig;* Design Architect: *Moore Ruble Yudell;* Principal-in-charge, Principal Designer: *John Ruble;* Principal Designer: *Charles Moore;* Principal Designer: *Buzz Yudell;* Project Manager: *Cecily Young; Mark Peacor, Curtis Woodhouse, Chris Duncan, John Taft, Craig Currie, Don Dimster;* Colour: *Tina Beebe;* Project Liaison: *J Miller Stevens*

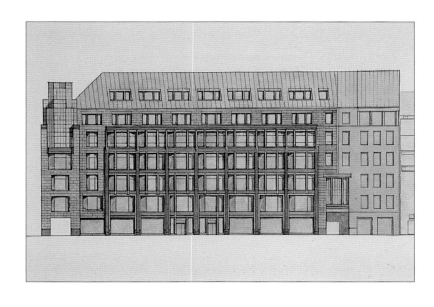

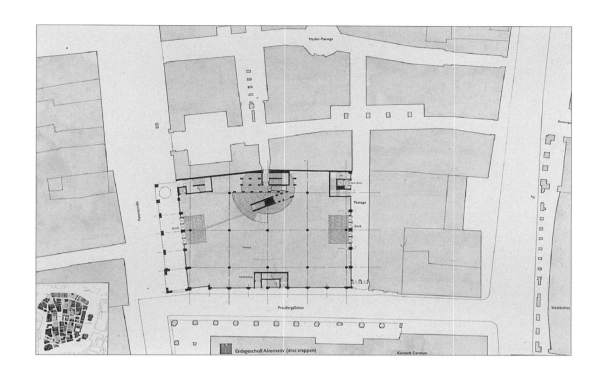

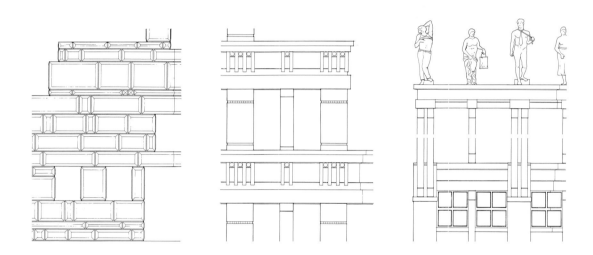

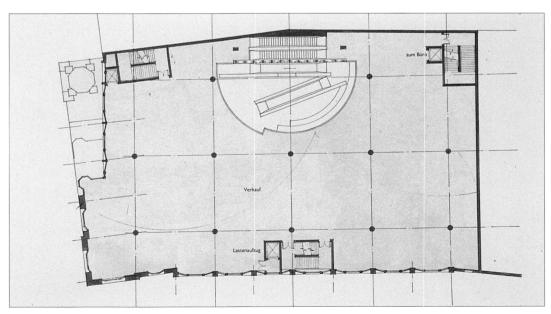

CENTRE: FACADE DETAILS

PLAZA LAS FUENTES
PASADENA, CALIFORNIA

Plaza Las Fuentes, a six-acre mixed-use development in the heart of Pasadena's historic district, includes new office space, retail space, hotel and conference facilities, and public gardens, designed and scaled carefully to reinforce the adjacent City Hall as a civic landmark and a focus of urban activity.

The configuration of the project seeks to fulfil the original city master plan, which set the City Hall as a civic jewel in the centre of a grand public garden. View corridors are carefully maintained, linking parts of the projects, especially its public gardens, to the City Hall. Major uses address City Hall and its civic neighbours, and buildings respect the existing street grid. A series of courts tie the life of this street pattern to the attractions of a new retail promenade and related gardens.

This promenade, a pedestrian street, stretches through the project, linking a series of courts. The heart of this sequence is a generous civic court located on axis with City hall. It is a central stage for the life of the project and a major public gathering place for Pasadena, suitable for outdoor performance. At the north end of the paseo *is a court giving access to a 360-room hotel and conference centre. The south end is anchored by office and restaurant uses. Between them, along the* paseo, *shops, fountains, restaurants and gardens will enliven the courts and*

arcades. The entire project encourages urban activity and invokes a spirit of celebration and variety.

The City required a connection to its tradition of Mediterranean architecture. The scale and design of the project take their cue from the adjacent City Hall. Arched arcades, deeply inset openings, stucco walls and tile roofs evoke the spirit of the region's architectural heritage in a fresh way, responding specifically to this particular site, context and time.

Owner: *Maguire Thomas Partners;* Design Architect: *Moore Ruble Yudell;* Principal-in-charge, Project Designer: *Buzz Yudell;* Principal Designers: *Charles Moore, John Ruble;* Proj. Director: *Daniel Garness;* Proj. Architect (Hotel): *Miguel Escobar;* Proj. Architect (Office/Retail/Plaza): *David Kaplan;* Technical Director: *Alfeo B Diaz; J Mary O'Connor, Cecily Young, Sylvia Deily, Hong Chen, Eugene Treadwell, James Wallace, George Venini, Mario Violich, Chris Kenney, Birgit Dietsch, Ying-Chao Kuo, Laura Gardner, Paul Boileau, Daniel Brooks, John Hotta;* Exec. Architects: *Gruen Associates;* Landscape Design: *Lawrence Halprin Assoc;* Master Planning Team: *Moore Ruble Yudell; Lawrence Halprin Assoc; Bartom Myers;* Landscape Production: *Omi Lang Assoc, Inc;* Interiors (Hotel): *Charles Pfister Assoc;* Interiors (Office): *Walker Assoc;* Graphics: *Sussman/Prejza;* Artwork: *Joyce Kozloff, Michael Lucero;* Colour: *Tina Beebe*

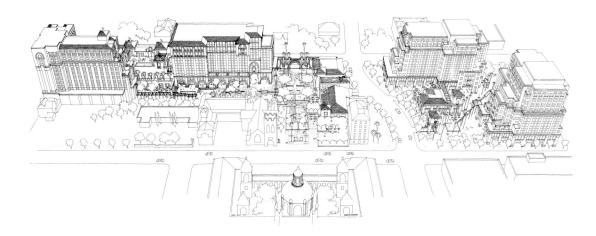

CENTRE: AERIAL VIEW

ABOVE AND BELOW: LOS ROBLES AVENUE ELEVATION; WALNUT STREET ELEVATION

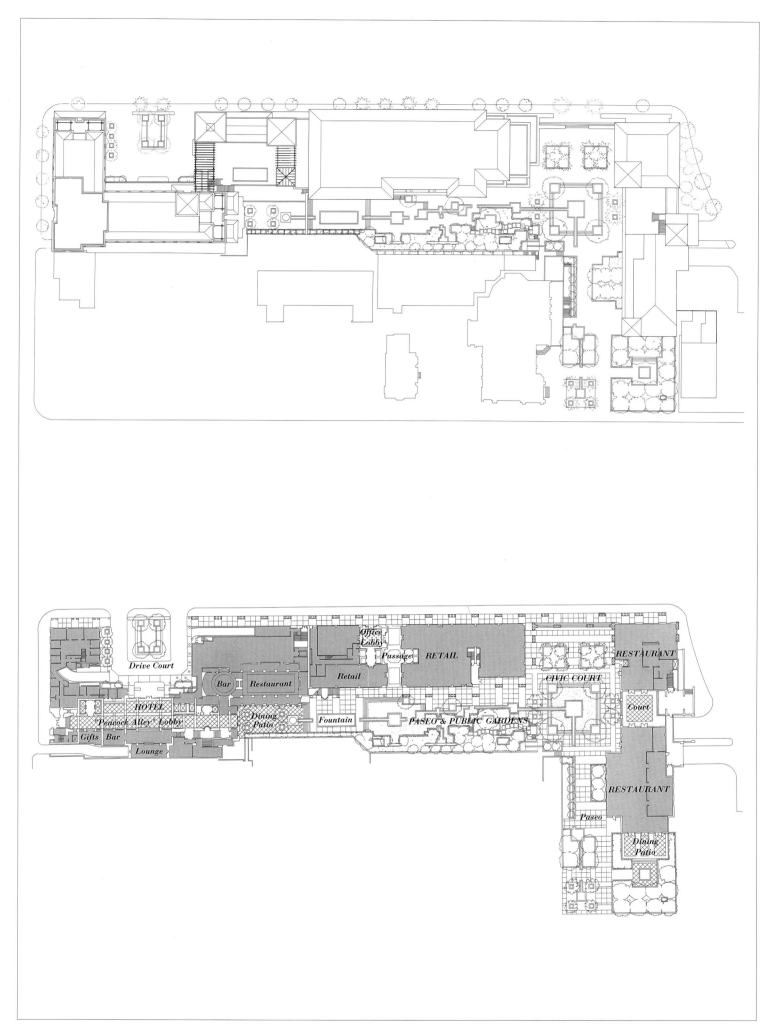

FROM ABOVE: REFLECTED ROOF PLAN; GROUND FLOOR PLAN

KIRCHSTEIGFELD COMPETITION, MARCH 1992
POTSDAM, GERMANY

As a result of the intense growth initiated since the reunification of Germany, this field located near to historic Potsdam is to be developed into a new town. The developer, in collaboration with the City of Potsdam, invited us to participate in a workshop for the master planning of the site. At the conclusion of the workshop, we were asked to collaborate with another participant, Rob Krier, for the further development of the master plan.

The site is fascinating. It represents a microcosm of the issues of development in East Germany since reunification: on one side, a small village, 700 years old, overrun by the sudden burgeoning of traffic through to Berlin; on another side, the Neues Siedlung, an all too common reminder of the brutalism of post-war planning; on the third side, the Autobahn, representing a positive link to the larger Germany, as well as the negative impacts of noise and pollution. Between them all sits Kirchsteigfeld.

For this fifty-three hectare site, we were asked to propose a plan for a new town to provide the full complement of civic, commercial, and residential uses, including 2,500-3000 units of housing, 160,000 square metres of commercial uses, two elementary schools, one high school, a sports centre and public parks and services.

Our approach was to plan a New Garden Village which seeks to offer the qualities of a small town by creating a sense of home and community for its inhabitants and visitors. Important issues considered were: earlier agrarian patterns, solar orientation, edges, axes, qualities of place, typologies, open spaces, walk-ability, neighbourhoods, streets as places. Ultimately, these issues coalesced into a multi-faceted approach, which featured several organising concepts: the weaving of an open

space network through and around the town; variety of housing and commercial typologies, and of densities of development; development of neighbourhoods or quarters, each with own centre and services; hierarchy of open spaces/spectrum of public to private; careful treatment of edges, relationships with neighbours, through careful massing and planning.

While our plan allows for considerable diversity of architectural treatment, it also establishes sequences of spatial experience ranging from discovery and surprise to grand procession. Likewise, the open spaces which make up the fabric of the public realm describe a spectrum from very intimate gardens to grandly scaled community gathering spaces. Each of the principal places in the plan are at this stage suggestive of character, but open to future interpretation. We hope to create planning principles which allow for orderly development, flexibility of phasing and the integration of a variety of architectural approaches. As in the richest examples of urban life, the whole should allow for diversity within harmony.

Design Architect: *Moore Ruble Yudell;* Principals-in-charge, Principal Designers: *John Ruble, Buzz Yudell;* Phase 1: Partners-in-charge: *Buzz Yudell, John Ruble;* Project Manager: *Shuji Kurokawa; A J Koffka, M Violich, J Mary O'Connor, S Gardner, D Garness, M B Elliot, L Bretana, A Padua;* Project Liaison: *Miller Stevens;* Competition: Project Manager: *Mark Peacor; C Young, M Violich, C Woodhouse, T Tran, R Destin, J Taft, C Currie, D Dimster, C Welch;* Participating Firms: *Augusto Romano Burelli; Eyl, Weitz, Würmle & Partner; Nielebock & Partner; Rob Krier and Partner; Moore Ruble Yudell; Krüger, Salzl, Vandreike, C Schuberth;* Renderings: *Al Forster*

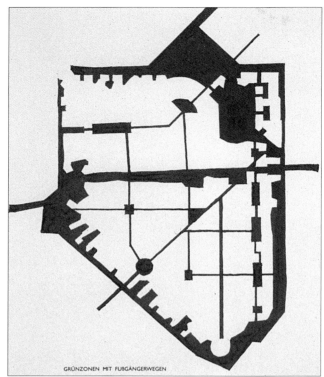

ABOVE FROM L TO R: CONNECTIONS FROM CONTEXT TO CENTRES WITHIN SITE; GREEN SPACE; NEIGHBOURHOOD CENTRE; WATER NETWORK

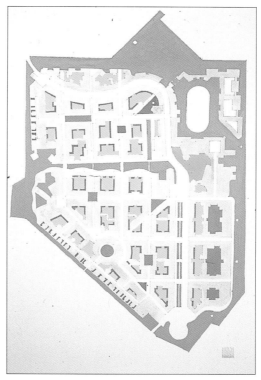

ABOVE FROM L TO R: BASIC DESIGN STRUCTURE; OPEN SPACE; FIGURE GROUND; SITE PLAN FINAL

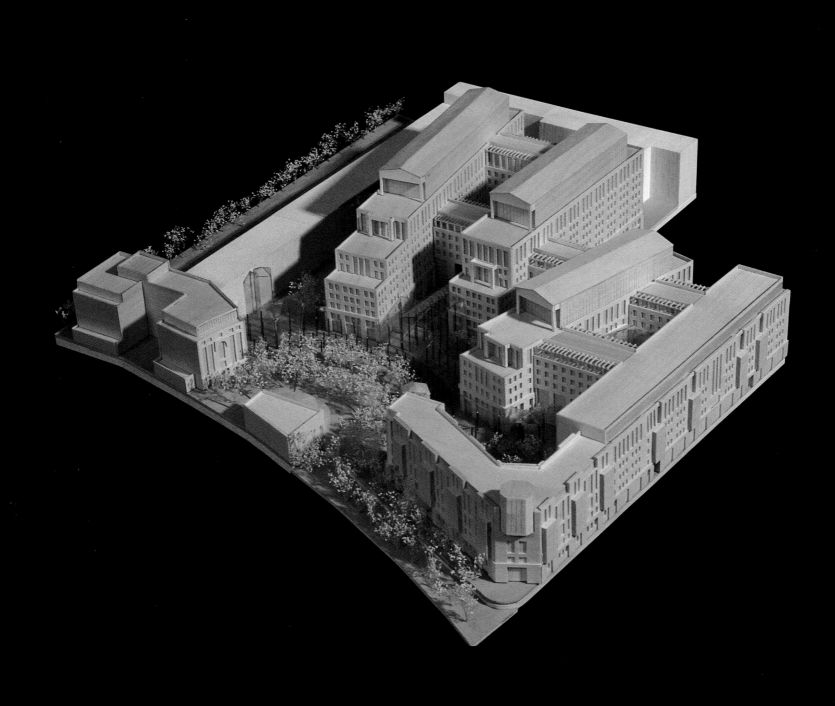

PROPOSAL FOR BOLLE CENTRE
BERLIN, GERMANY

A proposal for a mixed-use development in Berlin, near the Tiergarten and facing the Spree Canal, called for approximately 90,000 square metres of primarily new office space adjacent to an historical warehouse building, the Meierei. The site is entered by passing through large arcades in existing buildings along the Alt Moabit, a busy collector street. The scheme proposes four long, narrow buildings of seven, nine and eleven storeys loosely paralleling the Meierei, splayed slightly to suggest a centre point across the Spree. Each building steps with outdoor terraces to a winter garden greenhouse, curving in plan, containing cafés, shops, and indoor gardens. A major public plaza is shaped by a glassy colonnade and rows of trees; at its heart is a small restored industrial building against the Spree. Once the Meierei office, it is expanded here with canopies into a festival hall and café.

A new 100-unit housing block anchors the south-east corner along the Spree. The whole complex sits on one-and-a-half storeys of underground parking.

Our proposal recalls the strong unadorned vernacular of nineteenth-century industrial buildings and market halls: walls sheathed with brick and a generous use of steel and glass for atriums, lobbies and gathering places. The long stepped profile of the four buildings plus the Meierei make a skyline of glass temple-like façades and terraces from the Spree. The spaces between the buildings support a variety of active commercial and quiet garden uses. The central plaza presents a major event along the Spree, an urbane public park connected to the existing waterside pedestrian ways.

Project: *Bolle Competition;* Design Architect: *Moore Ruble Yudell;* Principal-in-charge, Principal Designer: *John Ruble;* Principal Designer: *Buzz Yudell;* Project Manager: *Daniel Garness; Mark Peacor, Tea Sapo, Curtis Woodhouse, John Taft, Chris Duncan, Sylvia Deily, Arlette Gordon, John Davis, Mario Violich*

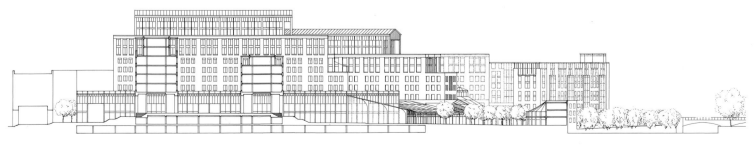

EAST SECTION

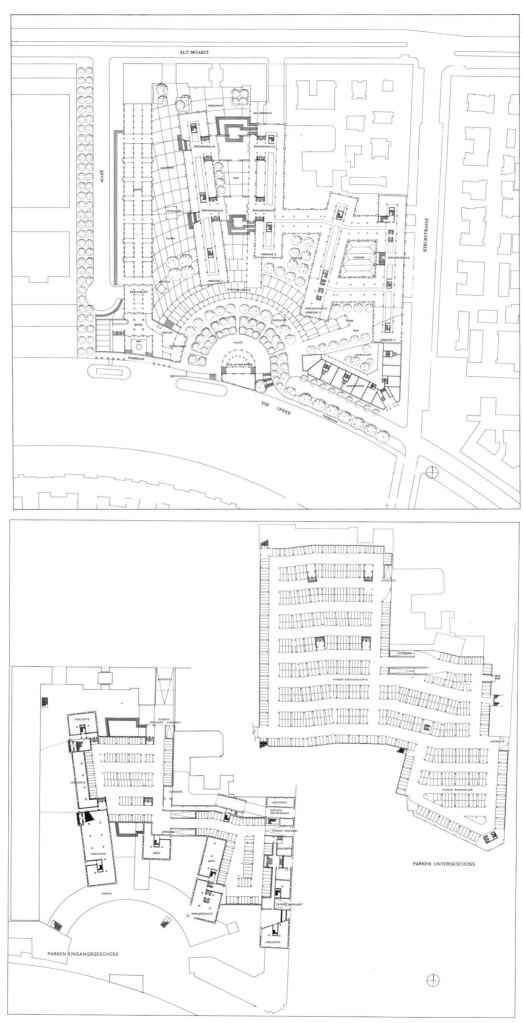

ABOVE AND BELOW L TO R: SITE PLAN; GROUND FLOOR PLAN; BASEMENT FLOOR PLAN

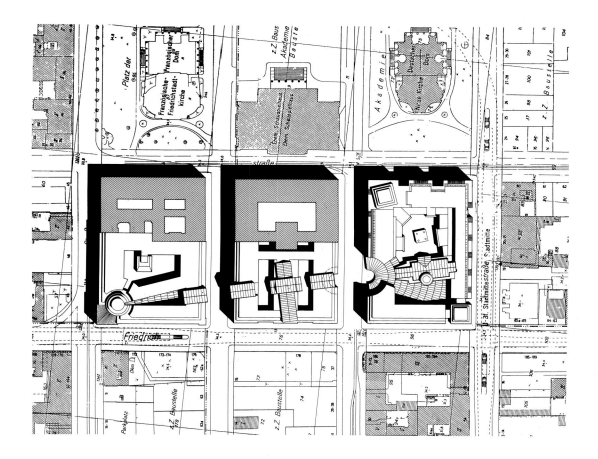

FRIEDRICHSTADT PASSAGEN
BERLIN, GERMANY

The challenge for our proposal for a three-block stretch at the heart of East Berlin was to set the tone for new urban development in the unified Germany. Located in the Berlin Mitte district adjacent to the historic Schauspielhaus and Akademieplatz, the site has been the focus of significant debate since reunification, resulting in the scrapping of an almost completed East German project there.

All three blocks are linked by a single pedestrian passage at street and concourse levels. This passage establishes a series of important public spaces within the project, without sacrificing maximum density for the surrounding uses. At the core of each block a principal room occurs along the passage that connects all levels of the passage vertically. Each one involves a thematic focus special to each block, a construction rising from the stone floor of the lower level. These pieces lend an immediate theatrical sense to the busy movement and arrival of people. In this, the traditional passage of pre-war Berlin is transformed into a contemporary forum for urban life.

The project includes a 225-room hotel overlooking Akademieplatz; ninety housing units on upper levels; 28,000 square metres of specialty retail; a department store; 63,000 square metres of office space; a fourteen-theatre cinema complex with food court; and at the rooftop level, looking out across the city, a city building museum for the display and discussion of future projects for Berlin.

Project: *Friedrichstadt Passagen;* Client: *Dumas West & Company, Brian Garrison;* Design Architect: *Moore Ruble Yudell;* Principal-in-charge, Principal Designer: *John Ruble;* Principal Designer: *Buzz Yudell;* Project Manager: *Cecily Young; Ying-Chao Kuo, Chris Duncan, Curtis Woodhouse, Arlette Gordon, John Davis, Doug Jamieson, Tony Tran, Keri Hogan, Anthony Tam;* Associated Architects: *Frank Williams & Associates, Frank Williams, Frank Uellendahl*

ABOVE: SITE PLAN

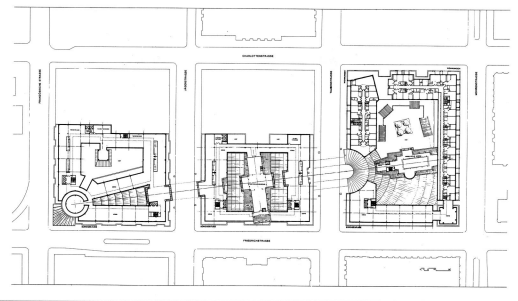

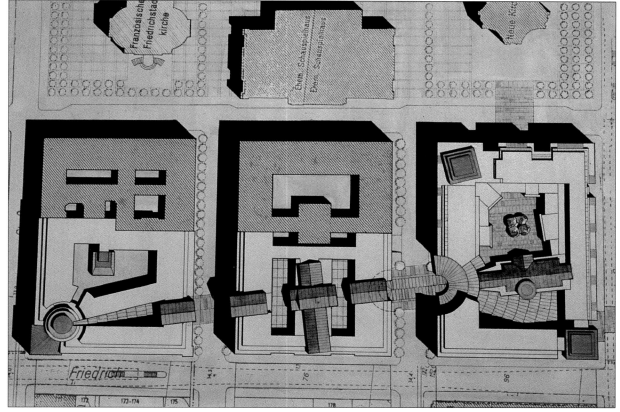

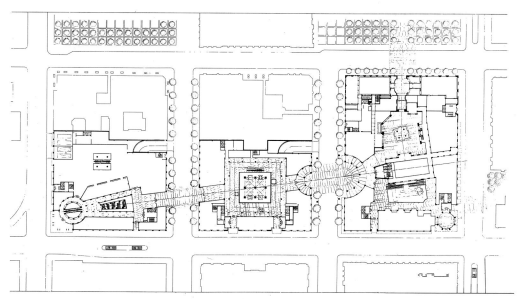

FROM ABOVE: SEVENTH TO EIGHTH FLOOR PLAN; ROOF PLAN; GROUND FLOOR PLAN

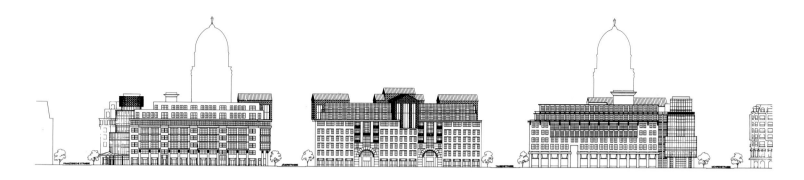

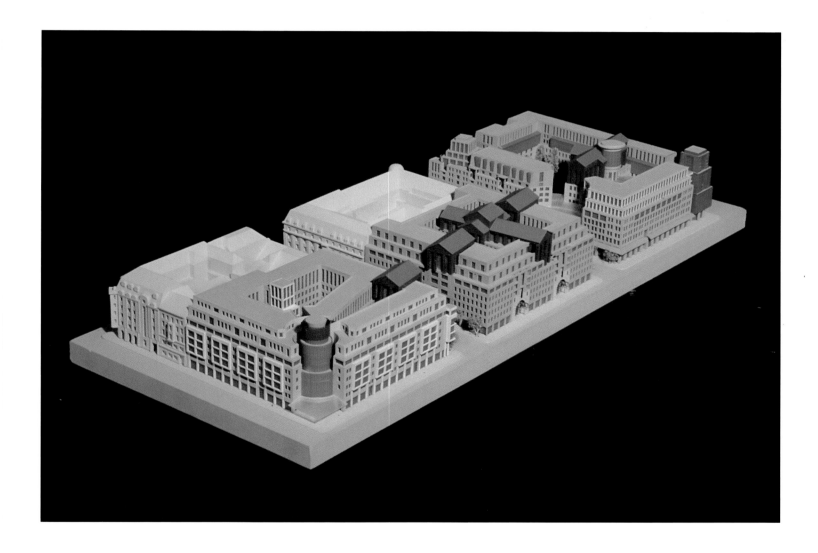

ABOVE AND BELOW: SOUTH ELEVATION; SECTION THROUGH PASSAGE

THE PARADOR HOTEL
SAN JUAN CAPISTRANO, CALIFORNIA

Our proposal for this 300-room hotel, which received First Prize in a 1982 design competition, carefully considered the developer's desired images: a centuries-old Mediterranean hillside village or fortress with a world of exotic gardens, courtyards and narrow streets to be discovered within. We wanted to evoke the picturesque by carving out places within a set of buildings that were simple, for economic reasons and strongly ordered, to maintain a sense of the whole.

The hotel occupies a hilltop, prominently visible at the edge of the San Diego Freeway and from the centre of the old town and Mission. The top of the site had been flattened; most of the building occurs at the edges of this plateau, with rooms to the quieter southern half and larger convention spaces perched on the north side, overlooking the highway. A nearly continuous spine-wall moves through the complex, connecting all the structures, top-lighting the double-loaded corridors of hotel rooms, emerging as a bridge and then sweeping out to terraces and courtyards in a grand arcade. Against this urbane, big-scale aqueduct plays the local colour of stucco and tile roof buildings. Water lilies and heady tropicals create the atmosphere of the public gardens. In a similar spirit, free-standing elevators in the lobby become towering palms of glazed terracotta.

Project: *The Parador Hotel;* Designer Architect: *Moore Ruble Yudell* (unbuilt project)

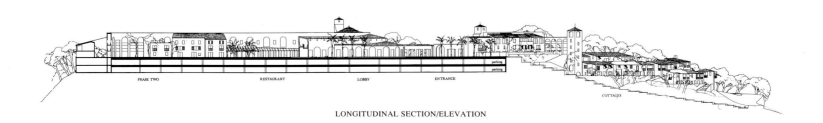

LONGITUDINAL SECTION/ELEVATION

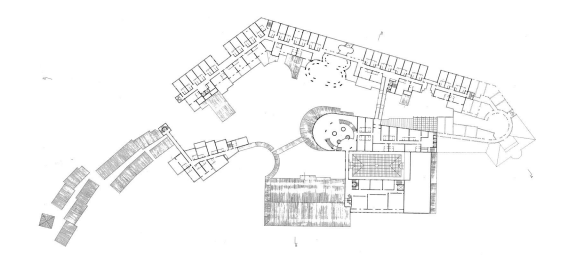

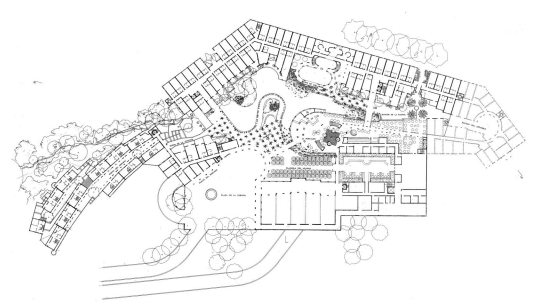

ABOVE AND BELOW: FIRST FLOOR PLAN; GROUND FLOOR PLAN

KNAPP CENTER
LOS ANGELES, CALIFORNIA

Our entry into this invited competition gave us the opportunity to explore the problem of an urban office building. The site, located on Wilshire Boulevard just across from the Los Angeles County Museum, is full of the kind of anomalies that occur in Los Angeles. While it is a key location on one of the city's major arteries, there is no consistent scale or building type in the immediate area. Although the entire Wilshire corridor is becoming lined with high-rise buildings, currently to the south of the site is a residential area of one to three storeys, and of three to four-storey commercial to the east. Across Wilshire is the museum's complex of buildings with a large addition.

We tried first to make a building which could live with these complexities, survive the anticipated increase in scale of the Wilshire corridor and reassert the importance of the street at this location. We also hoped to make a tower that had to do with Los Angeles history, landscape and climate. This seventeen-storey, 300,000 square-foot tower is organised simply in plan and uses a conventional glass curtain wall. It is shaped carefully to meet the street at a fairly low scale and steps up to a tower that has a strong image from a distance. The stepping form allows for numerous corner offices and roof gardens. At the street level, storefront entrances are articulated with a faceting that recalls older nearby buildings like Bullock's Wilshire. The north-west corner is a terraced plaza with fountains, cafés, and a grand stair down to parking levels.

In keeping with our concern for a practical commercial office building, the ornament of the building is developed with surface patterns of mullions and the use of coloured glass. Bands of grey and green, with a flourish of rose at the top, are sympathetic to the colours of local light and landscape.

Project: *Knapp Center;* Design Architect: *Moore Ruble Yudell* (Unbuilt project)

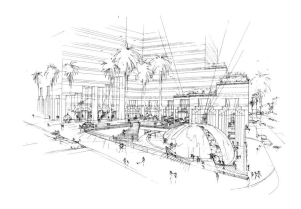

JOHN RUBLE
INTERVIEW BY JAMES STEELE

James Steele: Charles and Buzz have mentioned similar likes, dislikes, and sympathies in the architecture that you're engaged in. Where you began. How would you identify those?

John Ruble: To start with, I had only known Charles for a short time when we started the firm – actually, for about a year and a half. I'd always liked and admired his work. I think it's the fascination with different places and how ideas in architecture come from the experience of places, on the one hand, and also the whole collaborative side. Both of these appealed to me. We had just had a UCLA studio with Charles and for that we travelled to the Navajo Reservation. The free-wheeling field trip, the discussion about culture and place and the whole process of starting a design with real experiences of places rather than 'designing for mankind' were all very appealing. As we worked together professionally the different possible starting points for design work became broader, but it always had something to do with discovering specific notions of the place, or some piece of architecture that was intriguing.

JS: What is the process, in your view? Is it intuitive or analytical? How would you go about explaining what it is? Is it in finding what is specific about it?

JR: Well, a lot of times it can come down to site specific buildings that we like in the immediate context, or it can be that we study a collection of favourite buildings in the region—buildings that, for us, define the qualities of the region. What I think is good about it, is that it's not a very rigorous thing because we also feel free to import ideas, to bring something in from somewhere else that seems to have the right effect on a place. So there's quite a lot of freedom, but the intention somehow is always to make something recognisable. How to achieve this has evolved in the years we've been working. Buzz and I when we're working together probably do it a little differently than Charles and I when we're working together, or Buzz and Charles when they're working together, or all three of us. We all have different tendencies that result in different takes on these things.

JS: You believe it's an analytical process and intuitive process as well as a sympathetic process between you and the partner you're working with?

JR: Yes, but we do bring analysis into things. I think Buzz in particular is a strong influence in having the analytical lead to a kind of diagrammatic concept. He has a very strong commitment to that way of thinking. I am less immediately clear on some of those things than he is, but that's always a part of it. I think St Matthew's Church, on which all three of us worked, is quite picturesque, but evolved from a kind of analytical form-making. When it was time to put a roof on its plan, we had a semi-circular seating arrangement and knew that the congregation wanted the traditional 'Body of Christ' to form the nave and transept. It seemed also to require something else. I can't remember who initiated the idea of superimposing the Body of Christ over a hipped roof. But I would call that analytical in the sense of it being an abstraction of two well known, familiar forms. It's a formal idea which you can diagram very clearly and can be described in a single sentence, even though it didn't evolve from a linear thinking process – quite the opposite: it evolved from a collage of desires that came out of the workshops and it was left to us to sort those things out and make order out of them.

JS: In any partnership, no matter how close or sympathetic the partners are with each other, different people have different strengths to contribute to the partnership. I've been struck by the equality and democracy in the firm. Basically, I don't think that that's the way you really operate somehow. If that's the case, what would you say your strength is, and Buzz's and Charles' within this equality, and how would you characterise that if you had to?

JR: Well, I guess it's probably easier for me to talk about what their strengths are. I do think that there are some differences. Charles more often operates in the opposite direction from Buzz, in that he comes up with a specific idea about a form very quickly. Buzz would rather sneak up on a problem or talk about alternatives. I'm inclined to do it either way. One of my strengths is picking up on a certain direction and being able to take it a little bit further, or contribute an idea that somehow fits or relates to it. If left to my own devices, I head off in a fairly picturesque and romanticising direction. I think Buzz tempers that far more than I do with consistent rational thinking and formal clarity. Charles is capable of both things in extremes, and it's never clear which way he's going to be thinking on a particular day. What I admire about Charles is his fearless pursuit of what-the-central-issue-is, and his desire to give form to that issue, even if it's risky. I do think, though, that our work together is somewhat 'tougher' than what I see Charles doing with others. By 'tough' I mean that Buzz and I are willing to be quite abstract.

JS: Can you be more specific about that?

JR: 'Modern', for lack of a better word. Buzz looks increasingly for richness in the whole ensemble, more simple elegance in the parts and exuberance in the use of colour and light. Charles seems more willing to take forms and elements specifically out of history or vernacular architecture and use them with their full ornamentation in their most exuberant way. The UCSD Molecular Biology project is a good example: you can see a kind of tension between the over-all fabric of the building, and the conference-court which holds the centre as a rather elaborate set-piece. You can see us pulling in two directions at once, which makes the building an interesting document even though it might not be successful in every way. But I also think there's a 'consistent variety' in our work with strong visual connections to traditional forms. Generally speaking, people seem to associate us with that. I think we're always trying to push the limits of association with tradition. That's easy to see when you look at each project from the University of Oregon, to Tegel Harbour, to St Matthew's Church, to Nativity Catholic Church. Sometimes I'm surprised by how much consistency there is in these things.

JS: Do you characterise that consistency or credit that consistency to your interaction together?

JR: Yes. I think it's this 'extended family' loosely gathered around Charles, and involved in ideas that Sally Woodbridge once said have become 'community property' – not only for the three partners, but also for other people in the firm who work with us.

JS: What would those set of ideas be, if you had to make a list?

JR: First of all, roof and roof forms have been important. Oddly, our first house together didn't really have a roof. The Rodes House has a facade and you hardly notice its shed roof behind that. Nonetheless, most of the things we do, have a connection to vernacular or traditional building form, probably because they have roofs and modern architecture is noted for the fact that it doesn't show much of a roof. So it's a dead giveaway that we are often interested in deeply traditional building forms. The idea of having porches and of buildings to make streets and courts and other familiar kinds of places, the whole repertoire of city and campus and village place-making that we engage in, is a language that people who work with us are familiar with and are looking for new ways to do these things. In all of our work on campuses we find ourselves trying to recreate something that's been lost. But sometimes doing that with an individual building you can't always make a courtyard or a quadrangle, so you have to create the need for something.

JS: To generate a future.

JR: Yes. Or to lead to or set a precedent as it were.

JS: That's a very tricky process, isn't it?

JR: It can be, depending on the campus. At the University of Oregon it was very straightforward because we had a collection of buildings to do. There was the Christopher Alexander pattern language process, and a very handsome older campus. But where we were building origins of the campus had not been respected or continued, our game became to revitalise and to build on the older campus pattern of streets and courts. That we would feel was the right thing to do, even if Christopher Alexander hadn't mandated it. At the University of Washington, where we have just one building, there is a complex process of figuring out how the geometry of one thing is to support what was there and respect an overlay. The campus was a fascinating overlay of one plan after another made during the early twentieth century, leaving people with lots of choices today and lots to argue about. Our schemes were argued over by groups on campus quite a bit. We're pleased with the result because this one building addresses three campus places at once in a complex web of overlapping geometries, while it attaches to an existing building. So, working in many different places influences us in a way. Over time we become fluent with a whole repertoire of elements like the porches, towers, and terraces that connect with gardens and courts. Design has more to do with these connections and less about making a fascinating object.

JS: In terms of style, can you find affinities with other firms? Very few people are actually doing this kind of thing.

JR: There are a few firms that do. You would think we might feel affinity with people like Robert Stern, but we do distinguish our work as being less specific historically, even though we have a lot of appreciation for him. On the other hand, we're still searching for ways to respond to things in an evolutionary way, and our work varies over time. Obviously, we prefer not to be associated with Post-Modernism. I think it's unfair that Charles has been enshrined in that period. Looking at the Sea Ranch, for example, it's hardly fair to say he's a 'post-modern' architect by the normal definition of the word.

JS: Piazza d'Italia was the main criteria for that . . .

JR: It more or less defines Post-Modernism, doesn't it? But that's just it. We like to see our work as evolving and changing, even though we seem to have created some real post-modern icons. Tegel became one, and German architects and critics hate it, but the people who live there seem to love it.

JS: There is also this label 'pop architects' or 'pop architecture' that has been applied to you.

JR: Well, we are populists in a way. We put our foot down in terms of not wanting to be seen as avant-garde, and I think the whole posture of the current avant-garde is very limiting. Charles has said that the architects who can't hack the public involvement, can't do so because their egos aren't big enough. I don't know if that's the problem or not, but we do place a lot of credence in community; a sense of community and the idea of architecture being a manifestation of community and of habitation. We like to look at habitation in all its possible ways and see the people who will live in our buildings as having every right to be there during the design process. They're not just paying for the work. That's something we feel very strongly about and it shows in the workshops we do on so many projects.

JS: Are the workshops on-going?

JR: Yes. They've had a very strong influence on some projects, particularly on the campus projects at the University of Washington's Chemistry Building, and at Berkeley's Haas School of Business Administration. Those projects are strongly influenced and shaped by the ideas that came out of workshops. They show it in a way because they fit in – a process that's important. When we start thinking about places, one dimension is what the people who live there think about the place and that's part of the lore. People love certain buildings and hate others. Those things might change over time, but I think that in the long run people develop emotional attachments to places and they become important. That becomes part of understanding where you're building.

JS: How do you actually construct one of these workshops, or organise it? Is it a foregone conclusion that it's organised in a certain way?

JR: Well, you can see it as a crash course in design for a hundred and fifty, or two hundred lay people; or you can see it as an organised brawl. We've had workshops in public settings for community projects where at the first workshop people had to be separated and told to sit down. We've had others where everyone was very nice and it all came together beautifully and there was never a hint of controversy. But it all works because I think the activities are focused, organised and coherent.

JS: Who focuses those?

JR: Well, we do, based on the work we did with Jim Burns who co-invented this whole thing with Lawrence Halprin. We worked with Jim Burns on a number of occasions, and also evolved our own approach to these things.

JS: It's definitely a part of your process then?

JR: Not with everything, but where we can we propose participation with group and community clients. I think this kind of collaboration adds another dimension to the design process. It's a very important crossroads where different ideas come together and then the whole thing goes off in a certain direction. No one tells us how to detail a window, but they might say 'We want the central space of this business school to be here and not over here'. That, of course, has a huge effect on the design, but it may not effect the vocabulary of the building as such. However, the vocabulary of the building does evolve a little bit in the workshops. I think the workshop process is easily misunderstood in terms of what it means to the design. Anyone looking at it from the outside who hasn't done it, distrusts it. But it doesn't tell you what colour things should be or what proportional system to use. I guess I'm saying that we're still architects after the workshops are over.

JS: So it's a partnership between you and the people?

JR: Yes. There has to be a lot of trust. It doesn't substitute for clients trusting their architects.

JS: Did Kobe work that way?

JR: Kobe was, at times, a very arduous process of mutual education. It showed us how our Japanese clients worked. They had to give up the idea that the real estate department would just pick up the phone and tell the architects to make the building four storeys lower and get the drawings the next morning. It was a collaboration which took a lot of patience on both sides. It's lasted over the years and we have a strong relationship with the client now.

JS: You talked about evolution and the way the firm is changing. It's probably difficult to see where it's headed from your perspective, while in the midst of all this activity. Do you have any wishes for where it might go, or any vision of where it's headed?

JR: I think we've reached a point where there are things that we know how to do really well, like developing a complex of buildings such as housing, where 'traditional forms are skilfully recalled in modern terms'. I think our work is friendly – that is, accessible – but also involves quite a few surprises.

And I think we know how to make buildings that connect with gardens and give shape to formal places, courts and squares. We're learning a lot about that now. We've been working for a couple of years on the Playa Vista project; and recently in Berlin we've been doing some very interesting town planning work in collaboration with other architects like Rob Krier. We seek opportunities to get into town planning, where many interesting issues about community come up and where architecture is extremely important. This is informed by other concerns to do with the way our society builds big scale places over a relatively short period of time. Architecture has to turn to something like that because we've been through enough of the twentieth-century cycle of different kinds of invention and the whole ecological succession of style. It's like fashion design or many other things that change and produce new things but basically stay the same. We would like to take on these other problems: what towns will be like in the future and what cities will represent. Lately, the avant-garde architects see their work as some sort of shock therapy. But as American architects, we have a particular contribution to make, just because we want to make places that function for a community.

JS: LA is known for this 'shock therapy' and has this reputation. In a sense you're not part of the general trend here.

JR: No, I guess we've always been part of the romance of history. That's what people associate us with here. If you look at a project like the Nativity Church in Rancho Santa Fe, there's no question that it's part of the California mythology of the missions, the point of which seems to be a concentrated community space as a focal element in the landscape. However abstract in form, we are still drawn to these archetypal starting points. If everybody else wants to stray from those things for a while, that's fine too. But our interest in the on-going invention of modernism is no less passionate than that of other people more associated with it. In our case it's more a matter of the details using light, colour and so on.

JS: How does that work in with Playa Vista? It's a large project, one of your largest, and you're working with other people on it.

JR: Playa Vista is a great example of collaboration. If you allow other people their contribution and you're open, you don't always agree every time. However, we've found that we've been fortunate to be involved in teams where there's a great deal of sympathy. There's a fair amount of overlap and enough difference in experience or expertise that there really is a fresh contribution on all sides. I think we have a lot in common with Laurie Olin and Bob Hanna, the landscape people working on Playa Vista, in terms of our thinking about cities and places; but they have a whole other experience and awareness. It's the same with Jan Wehberg and Cornelia Müller, the landscape architects we've worked with in Berlin, who have a great depth of appreciation for the history of what has been made there and a modern kind of insight into that. Whenever we've had these kinds of chances to collaborate, I think it works well. It comes to a point where you want to collaborate on certain common ground and then to be free to each do your thing.

JS: Was there any study of California or LA typologies at Playa Vista?

JR: Yes. Mostly courtyards and courtyard houses, but not much in the way of single family individual housing, because in Playa Vista there really aren't any. None of the housing projects that we've done have involved real single family housing. But we often use a villa typology with anywhere from six to fourteen units in each house.

JS: Was that true at Tegel?

JR: Tegel had around six, I think. They have a nice way of defining the town edge of the site, but leave a sense of openness.

JS: Do you find you work a lot with developers?

JR: Yes. That's about a third of our effort and at times it's much more. We've been fortunate to work with developers who have a great sense of their role in the community. Nonetheless, they have a bottom line you eventually come up against. It's naive to think you can work with a developer and never fight over anything. On the other hand, when the fighting is over and everybody has worked something out it's very satisfying. We're very keenly aware of the successes and the losses as we go through that process. At the end of the project, I think hopefully people don't notice that so much. They see something which works and has a certain validity.

JS: Plaza Las Fuentes was one of the situations, wasn't it?

JR: Yes, a typical overlay of city, developer, architect, where all three are in the ring together. It's a multiple alliance, and has conflicts sometimes, but we find ourselves being agents of bringing all interests together. Perhaps all three parties see themselves in this way. But, we're really the agency that does this, because in the end I think people look at what's built and don't first think about how much it cost. They first think, 'Does it work? Is this a good place or not'. The work that the architect and the builders do is what everyone judges. So I think we're the ones who have to ultimately satisfy the interests of these various groups and create an architecture that expresses our common values.

ST MATTHEW'S EPISCOPAL CHURCH
PACIFIC PALISADES, CALIFORNIA

The Parish of St Matthew viewed the destruction of their church by fire in 1978 not simply as a loss, but as the opportunity to bring the church community together in the act of building anew. We were given the exciting charge by the vestry to involve the parish fully in the planning and design of the church. Further, the schematic design would need to be approved by a two-thirds vote of the parish.

In four monthly workshops, members of the congregation collaborated with us on decisions from siting the building to determining its size, facilities, layout and budget. More than 200 parishioners participated in this process and the schematic design achieved an approval of eighty-seven per cent of the congregation. The workshops evolved as a forum in which diverging views were synthesised. Many parishioners wanted, for acoustic and liturgical reasons, a lofty symmetrical church with a minimum of glass and wood. Another group spoke for a more informal and rustic building with intimate seating, views to the old prayer garden, extensive use of wood and a close relationship with the benign outdoors of Southern California.

The building evolved in close response to these issues as workshop participants modelled the options. Passing under low and informal porches one enters through a glass narthex to a lofty formal nave. Here, liturgical processions are framed by arches of ornamented steel that carry the major structural supports. The traditionally configured nave and transept intersect a large hipped roof, carved away in deference to favourite trees and to make courtyards and a cloister. Seating for 350 congregants is made intimate by its curved plan, allowing everyone to

be within seven rows of the altar.

To accommodate the desire for wood, without sacrificing acoustics, a system of wall battens was developed on walls of structural steel frame with four inches of plaster. Windows are minimised in the nave and located to frame views of the prayer garden, while a small adjoining chapel is made especially transparent for its connection to the outside. Energy-conscious parishioners suggested operable skylights at the ridge. These and the building volume obviate the need for air conditioning, while the climate allows for minimal heating. The exterior of the building is stucco with expansion joints composed to recall the 1920s half-timbered stucco of the nearby Founder's Hall.

We feel that the success and excitement of the building lies in it demonstrating that the open participation of a community can produce a building as sensitive to its time and place as can any effort of the architect alone. The building can be a specific creation of the community while the architects, as partners, lose none of their importance as makers of form and place.

Project: *St Matthew's Episcopal Church;* Owner: *Parish of St Matthew;* Design Architect: *Moore Ruble Yudell;* Principal-in-charge, Principal Designer: *John Ruble;* Principal Designer: *Charles Moore;* Principal Designer: *Buzz Yudell;* Project Manager: *J Timothy Felchlin; Jason Balinbin, Robert Flock, Andra Georges, Shinji Isozaki, David Kaplan, David Kellen, Peter Zingg;* Planning Consultant: *Jim Burns;* Lighting: *Richard C Peters;* Landscape: *Campbell and Campbell;* Acoustics: *Purcell + Noppe;* Stained Glass: *Jane Marquis;* Colour: *Tina Beebe*

LEGEND

1	NAVE	9	LIBRARY
2	CHOIR	10	CLERGY
3	ALTAR	11	SACRISTY
4	NARTHEX	12	CLOISTER
5	BAPTISTRY	13	BELL TOWER
6	CHAPEL	14	COURTYARD
7	CHOIR PRACTICE	15	COVERED WALKWAY
8	ACOLYTES	16	MECHANICAL

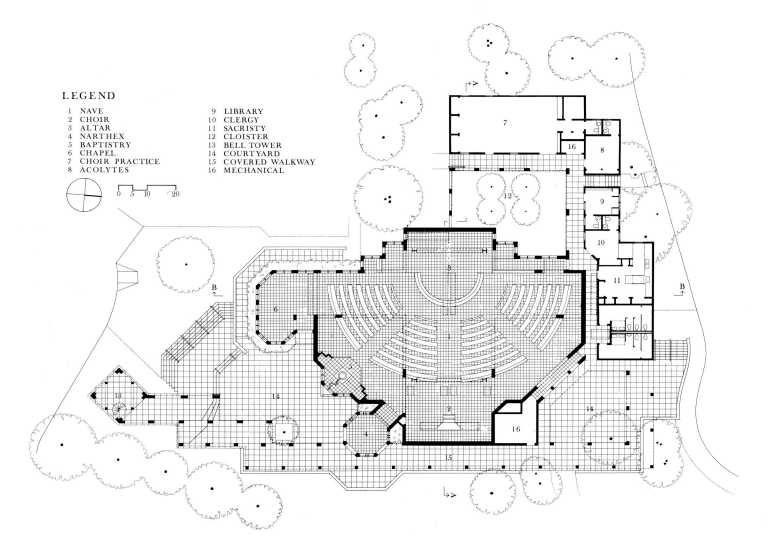

CENTRE: GROUND FLOOR PLAN

FROM ABOVE: SOUTH-WEST ELEVATION; WEST ELEVATION; EAST ELEVATION

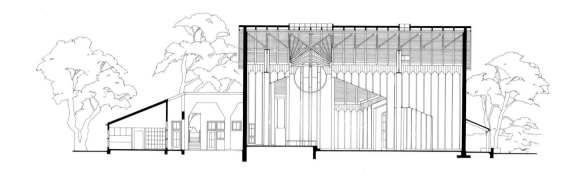

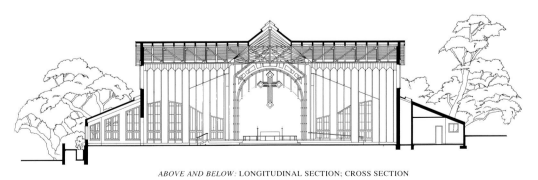

ABOVE AND BELOW: LONGITUDINAL SECTION; CROSS SECTION

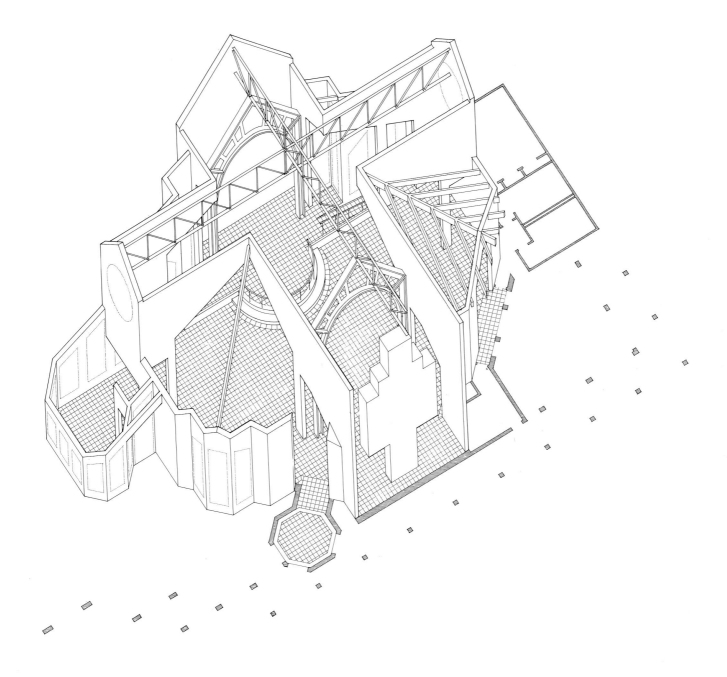

FIRST CHURCH OF CHRIST, SCIENTIST
GLENDALE, CALIFORNIA

Two Christian Science congregations in a small, prosperous southern California town united to build a new church. A small site made accommodation of programme and parking requirements a challenge.

Our approach was to group the various uses around a courtyard through which the main auditorium, Sunday School building, offices and meeting rooms are all entered. Arrival from the parking areas on two levels is at one corner, marked by a tower that brings light down a stairwell to the lower level. The entrance to the foyer of the auditorium is at the opposite corner of the courtyard, extending to it the sequence of movement. The foyer itself is a glassy bay that brings the courtyard in and creates, in the evening, a glowing pavilion of light along the street.

The auditorium seats 250 people. It is filled with filtered clerestory light and offers views onto two small gardens, protected by generous gables, and out through large openings that recall the Arts and Crafts tradition of the region's architectural heritage. The central aisle of the auditorium runs on the diagonal, increasing the sense of spaciousness and focusing attention on the readers' podium. The wall behind the podium is coloured subtly, washed with sunlight from a hidden skylight. Wood latticework articulates further the focus of the room, extend-

ing to screen the pipes of the organ.

The Sunday School building, across the courtyard from the auditorium, has a nursery and a flexible Sunday School area that can be used for large gatherings, yet it offers privacy to smaller groups. Ancillary meeting rooms and offices complete the enclosure of the courtyard on three sides; while on the fourth, broad steps and a ramp open out to the street. The courtyard works as the outdoor heart of the church, encouraging informal gatherings.

The Arts and Crafts tradition evoked by the design of the church is realised in simple materials – walls are painted board and batten, roofs are composition shingle. A small site and limited budget have not hindered the creation of a tranquil, memorable church that is responsive to its place, its tradition, and its congregation.

Project: *First Church of Christ, Scientist;* Owner: *First Church of Christ, Scientist, Glendale;* Design Architect: *Moore Ruble Yudell;* Principal-in-charge, Principal Designer: *John Ruble;* Principal Designer: *Charles Moore;* Principal Designer: *Buzz Yudell;* Project Manager: *George Nakatani;* Head of Production: *Alfeo B Diaz; Aileen Schier, Hong Chen, Mark Denton, Steve Gardner, Ying-Chao Kuo, Neal Matsuno, Eugene Treadwell;* Landscape: *Nancy Goslee-Power;* Colour: *Tina Beebe*

WEST ELEVATION

LONGITUDINAL SECTION

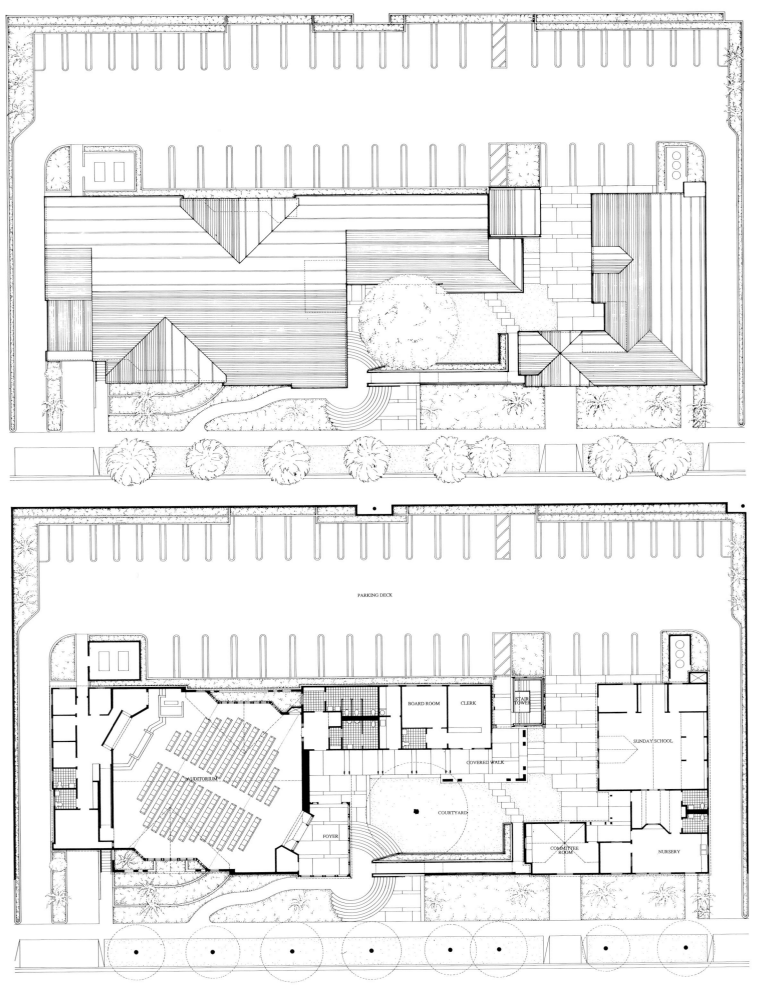

PARKING DECK

BOARD ROOM CLERK STAIR TOWER

SUNDAY SCHOOL

COVERED WALK

AUDITORIUM

COURTYARD

FOYER

COMMITTEE ROOM NURSERY

FROM ABOVE: ROOF PLAN; GROUND FLOOR PLAN

NATIVITY CATHOLIC CHURCH
RANCHO SANTA FE, CALIFORNIA

In a rural valley north of La Jolla, our client's vision was to found, like the early California missionaries, a parish around which a Christian community would develop. The new buildings form a walled compound set back from the road to create a sense of a place apart, yet open to the community. A dirt road on axis with the church building leads through a grove of trees to the main cloister.

Within the walls, the church, parish hall, rectory, four chapels and columbarium orient inwards in Spanish-Mexican tradition. Their placement creates a series of cloisters and gardens, layered to establish a sequence of spaces that culminates in the place of worship.

The church, a longitudinal nave with a single transept, offers semi-circular seating for 550. The altar wall intersects the crossing; large openings at its two ends wash the walls with indirect sunlight. Ambulatories, aisles, shrines

and choir evoke ecclesiastical architectural tradition, separated from the nave by columns and screens.

Future plans include a school, sited behind the church compound and linked to it by porches, gardens and courts.

Project: *Nativity Catholic Church;* Owner: *Diocese of San Diego;* Design Architect: *Moore Ruble Yudell;* Principal-in-charge, Principal Designer: *John Ruble;* Principal Designer: *Charles Moore;* Principal Designer: *Buzz Yudell;* Project Manager: *Renzo Zecchetto; Alfeo B Diaz, Patrick Ousey, Michael de Villiers, James Mary O'Connor, Brian Tichenor, Hong Chen, Erick Mikiten, Neal Matsuno, George Venini, Steve Gardner;* Associated Architect: *The Austin Hansen Group:* Principal-in-charge: *Randy Robbins;* Production Architect: *Karl Ponath;* Landscape: *Moore Ruble Yudell with Austin Hansen Group;* Lighting: *Richard C Peters, Neal Matsuno;* Colour: *Tina Beebe*

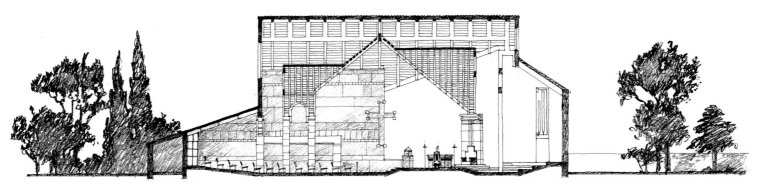

CROSS SECTION

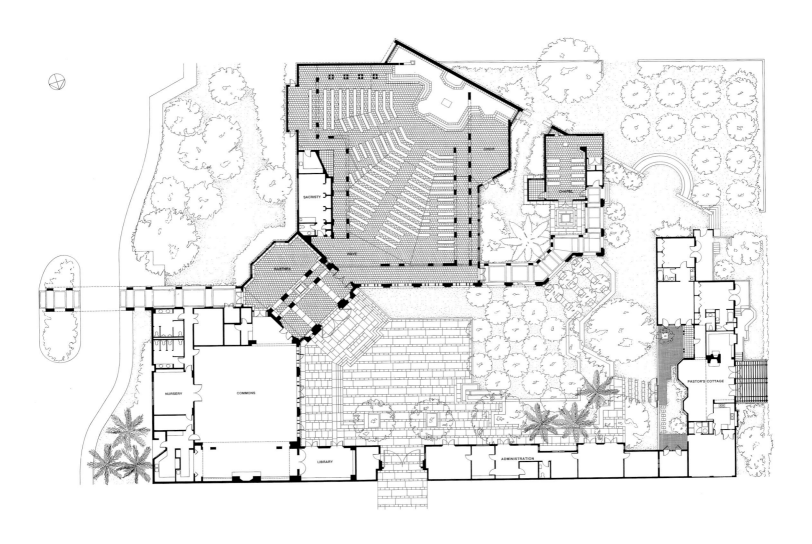

SACRISTY

NARTHEX

NURSERY

COMMONS

LIBRARY

ADMINISTRATION

CHAPEL

PASTOR'S COTTAGE

PLAN OF WALLED COMPOUND

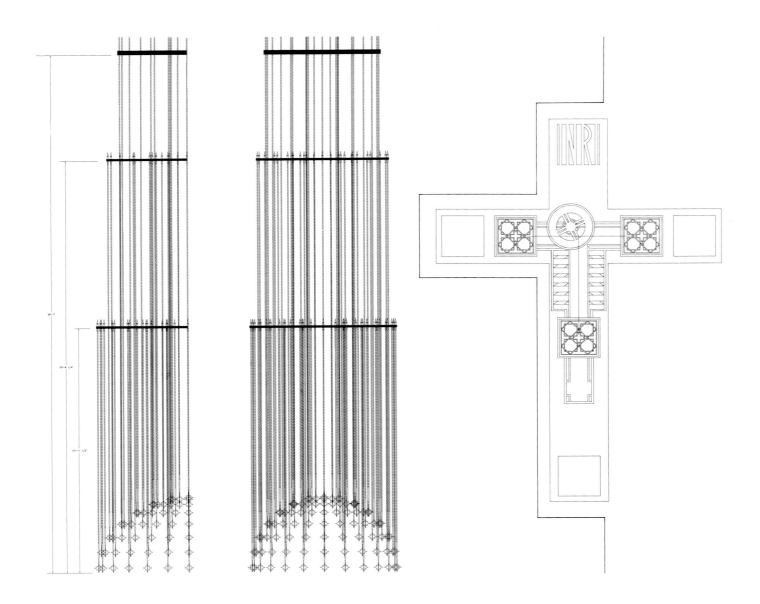

BALDACCHINO, SIDE AND FRONT ELEVATIONS; CRUCIFIX DETAIL

BODY MOVEMENT

BUZZ YUDELL

The interplay between the world of bodies and the world of our dwelling places is always in flux. We make places that are an expression of our haptic experiences, even as these experiences are generated by the places we have already created. Whether we are conscious or innocent of this process, our bodies and our movements are in constant dialogue with our buildings.

There is, perhaps, no clearer and more powerful image of our relation to the forms built with our own hands than the caryatids of ancient Greek temples. These young maidens, carrying the weight of ornamented and inhabited entablature and pediment, stand serenely, seemingly unburdened by the transfer of a great load. They establish the link between earth and sky, between the rocks upon which they stand and the gods whose lives are recorded in the pediment. Nor are they static or frozen in this role: undaunted by their special burden, the caryatids express the potential for movement – with raised knee, they are ready to venture with ease and certainty into the space of their mortal world. This image of humankind carved into architecture affirms our place in the world.

As with the caryatids, our movements are ever subject to the same physical forces as built forms and may be physically contained, limited, and directed by these forms. Inevitably, they are entwined more intricately with and dependent upon architecture than are the sound and notation expressions of conversation, song, music, and writing. This critical interaction of body form and movement with architecture deserves careful attentions.

The Spatiality of Movement

It is not surprising that forms are more often the focus of our attention than space, or movement in space. Space is thought of typically as a void or as the absence of solid; movement is thought of as a domain separate from its existence in space.

We can look to the dancer for some fresh sense of these realms. Dancers speak of 'feeling' space. This ether through which most of us look, focusing on solid objects, becomes real 'stuff' to the dancers. Martha Graham, the doyenne of modern dance in this country, would regularly base a set of exercises on the haptic experience of space. Her students were asked to hold, push, pull, and touch pieces of space and places in space. A natural outcome of this kind of training is that the entire body is mobilised gradually to touch and feel space, so that movement

becomes not a vague indescribable set of reflex actions, but an articulately felt interaction with the positive stuff of space. The dancer and the space animate one another as partners.

If dancers feel a critical relationship to the space outside their bodies, they also sense an essential relationship to the inside. In forms as divergent as classical ballet and modern dance, the practitioners speak of the constant need to find or feel one's 'centre'. This centre must be felt before the dancer can confidently move in space, the outside. This is, indeed, reminiscent of our need to sense the security inside our dwelling place in order to act with strength in the outside community.

A vital aspect of the dancer's maintenance of a sense of body centre while moving in space is the continuous awareness of the pull of gravity. This omnipresent force that we seldom consider consciously is the object of the dancer's acute awareness. Dancers' responses to gravity have been varied but always intense, almost obsessive. Ballet has developed, in part, as the art of denying gravity: years of technical training are devoted to creating the illusion of effortless leaps and flutters through space. With contrary intention but an equally powerful response, much of modern and folk dance displays and celebrates the pull and power of the earth with actions of falling, stomping, and embracing the ground. In one of the revolutionary acts of early modern dance, Mary Wigman scandalised German audiences by bumping her way across the stage on her back, feet, and hands. In this performance of 1919 she was saying that gravity, the earth, and down are real and that we are bound inevitably by such powers.

This 'centre' is not a concept of geometry but one of the musculature with all its kinesthetic ramifications, of orientation in response to the pull of gravity, and of a sense or feeling of inside.

Looking at the body in space, we find that geometric abstractions and descriptions quickly assume layers of associative meaning. Rudolf Laban, an influential pioneer in graphic notation for dance, described movement in terms of the 'frontal', 'vertical' and 'horizontal' planes, providing a tri-axial structure remarkably similar to the psycho-physical co-ordinates of the body-image theorists. A look at the vertical and horizontal dimensions is especially relevant to movement in architectural space.

The standing figure becomes a symbol as well as an element of the vertical axis. As the implicit link

Ziggurat buildings of earlier New York zoning laws invite us to people their landscape

Sheer prisms give us 'shafts'

Opposite: *Pinnacles of the Chrysler Building, New York*

Citizens in action in King's Dream of New York, *1908*

Tatlin's Monument to the Third International *(1919-20) spirals diagonally*

between earth and sky, he or she becomes the communication between the two realms. And because these realms have radically different properties, the body becomes the matrix for the synthesis and resolution of this polarity. Up and the sky are divine, spiritual, ethereal, light, rarefied, spreading, a canopy. Down and the earth are material, mineral, dark, compact, firm, a solid, a cave.

Movement upwards can be interpreted as a metaphor of growth, longing, and reaching; and movement downward as one of absorption, submersion, and compression. Since the images of womb and tomb are associated with the earth, and images of resurrection and the afterlife are related to the sky, the vertical axis is also bound closely to the concept of transition through the cycles of life.

In contrast, movement in the horizontal plane relates only to the earthly stage in that cycle. Laban has identified this plane as the zone of communication and social interaction. The communication or change, however, is not related to the personal longing which is associated with the vertical axis.

All human movement traces complex spatial configurations. Its forms can be seen as a compounding of movements through the spatial axes – a process continually changing in time. Curvilinear and diagonal motions are developed in relation to the two axes, while spiral and helical motions are developed in relation to three axes. It is interesting to note that movement in two axes or one plane, such as walking, running, and most forms of human locomotion, is the most prevalent mode in a typical day's activities. Movement in one dimension, such as diving into the water (a very rightly defined and restricted movement), and movement relative to three dimensions, such as the baseball player's wind-up (a very spatially complex and dynamically changing movement), are both exceptions to our normal patterns.

Although we are capable of an infinite range of movements, most of us move within a fairly narrow range of our possible spectrum. One of the critical determinants of this range is the built environment: the spaces and stuff that we construct and inhabit.

The Building as a Stimulus for Movement

All architecture functions as a potential stimulus for movement – real or imagined. A building is an incitement to action, a stage for movement and interaction, one partner in a dialogue with the body.

We need only to recollect our own childhood activities to see how easily sparked is the haptic interaction of body form with built form. Consider the simple game of stepping on every crack in the sidewalk. Here the child plays his body (its dimensions, shapes, and rhythms) against the given grid of the sidewalk paving. Usually the chance cracks are integrated into the game, thus complicating the time and movement patterns that are developed. Or consider the game of hopscotch. Here a bilaterally symmetrical chalk grid is the 'structure' with which

the body plays. Variations in the speed, rhythm, and dynamic of the movement are rather simply induced by the configuration of the grid: fast, less stable movement through the single-box-one-leg hops; slower, more controlled and balanced movement through the double-box-two-leg manoeuvres; and jump turns at the ends of the grid. In both games the body is stimulated by the physical pattern into an interaction which generates a kind of spontaneous primitive dance. It is an experience almost all of us have shared and of which we are still capable.

Another common experience also shares these characteristics: running a stick along a picket or cyclone fence. The regular periodic spacing of the pickets or steel wire is the 'Cartesian' given of the built environment. The rhythmic variables are the speed and pacing with which the child or 'musician' moves against the grid. Here a kind of music is the product, and the importance of both the animate and inanimate participants is heightened.

The ebbs and flows, weights, rhythms, and surges that emanate from us are inherent in the body and its movements. Try to walk in precise and even measures. Even if you succeed in doing so horizontally, as in a march, there will still be complex rhythmic events in the vertical dimension (the raising and lowering of the chest with breathing and the changes in the relative alignment of body weight), not to mention the internal rhythms of heart and pulse.

Given this rhythmic richness that we all possess, and the fact that patterns as mundane as pavement cracks and picket fences can elicit complex haptic responses, we might well wonder why any building cannot be as good as the next in generating a body response. Why are we not moved by our neighbourhood shopping mall or city centre office tower? Take, for example, a typical curtain-wall skyscraper. Its potential for pulling us into the realm of a movement or sound game is almost nil. We can neither measure ourselves against it nor imagine a bodily participation. Our bodily response is reduced to little more than a craned head, wide eyes, and perhaps an open jaw in appreciation of some magnificent height, or of some elegantly prescribed mullion detailing.

Compare this with a 1930s ziggurat skyscraper, such as the Chrysler building. Here we have not only the vertical differentiation of the building, but chunky setbacks which conjure landscapes or grand stairways. We can imagine scaling, leaping, and occupying its surface and interstices. Even the cheap and efficient stepped-back curtain-wall buildings erected along New York City's Park Avenue in the 1950s and 1960s provide us with some form of imagined cubic landscape, in spite of their forfeiture of body relation at smaller scale and at street level. A section through a street flanked by ziggurat buildings yields the 'canyon', quite different from the tight, unpenetrated slot that the sheer curtain-wall towers produce. By these we are given not the 'canyon' but the 'shaft', and the difference in imagery is signifi-

Insidious Strains of Futurism

In the hands of a brilliant craftsman like Mies van der Rohe, a spatiality of alienation may still provide its rewards through the elegance of material and construction. But the more extreme applications of Cartesian space present an insidious threat to our identity as individuals. The futurist group Superstudio has given us some of the most haunting images of bodily alienation. One of their visions promises the total freedom of living on an infinite gridded platform into which we may plug for energy, information, or nutritive needs. We are assured that in this Utopia we shall no longer require clothes or shelter and that we can be transported in an instant to any part of the earth. This scenario embodies a clear denial of the need for the interaction of body and architecture. There are no landmarks, no stimuli, no stages, and no centres.

The other extreme to alienation of the body is over-manipulation of the body. The two are often complimentary phenomena, and it is not surprising that this hyper-manipulation is in the domain of some of the same futurists who would have us be neutralised nomads, unhinged from our special places. Members of the Archigram group have proposed such future pleasures as *Manzak*:

All the sensory equipment you need for environmental information retrieval, and for performing tasks. Direct business operations, do the shopping, hunt or fish, or just enjoy electronic instamatic voyeurism, from the comfort of your own home.

And the *Electronic Tomato*:

For the great indoors, get instant vegetable therapy, from the new Electronic Tomato – a groove gizmo that connects to every nerve end to give you the wildest buzz.

These are surely images of the manipulation and electronic co-option of our bodies and their initiative. It is total passivity. Our bodies are circuited out of our existence as our world is realised in electronically stimulated sensation.

Originally written with Charles Moore and Kent Bloomer as a chapter of Body Memory and Architecture, *published by Yale University Press, 1975.*

Richard Upjohn, Connecticut State Capitol

Archigram, Electronic Tomato

Opposite: *University of California Faculty Club, Santa Barbara;* Left: *Connecticut State Capitol*

233

RODES HOUSE
LOS ANGELES, CALIFORNIA

This house was designed for a bachelor English professor who wanted a serene and formal home on a modest budget. The house evolved from the limitations of its site – a flat, trapezoid-shaped orchard with hills rising steeply on two sides. The orchard is loose-fill and unbuildable. The only way the house could meet its low budget was to span the hill.

This span was first designed with trusses within the exterior walls. It then evolved into a series of three trussed bridges which pierced the long symmetrical curve of the façade, the inner wall of the living room and the rear of the dining room conservatory. In the final scheme, the truss construction was not affordable and the span was achieved with a buried bridge of caissons and grade beams. The owner and the architects took such pleasure in the play of the straight trusses and the curved façade that it is recollected with a plane of light-weight lattice that invites vegetation and serves as an armature for lighting.

In a very small house the gourmet owner wanted

generous provisions for cooking and dining, and a grand living room. In order to save space he was content to settle for an alcove bed in the style of Thomas Jefferson's. Upstairs a guest room and bath are across the bridge from a small study.

In front of the house there is an oval patio that serves as a stage for performers visiting the client's university, while guests sit in an orange grove laced with fragments of a terraced amphitheatre. Modest materials, stucco exteriors and plaster interiors are animated by pastel walls and vegetation. For the owner and the architects, special pleasures of the house exist in its response to both the apparent and hidden qualities of the site.

Project: *Rodes House;* Owner: *David Rodes;* Design Architect: *Moore Ruble Yudell;* Principal-in-charge, Principal Designer: *Buzz Yudell;* Principal Designer: *Charles Moore;* Principal Designer: *John Ruble; J Timothy Felchlin, Regula Campell, Jim Meyer;* Colour: *Tina Beebe*

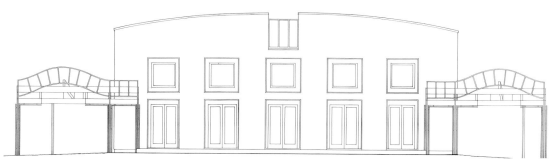

FRONT ELEVATION

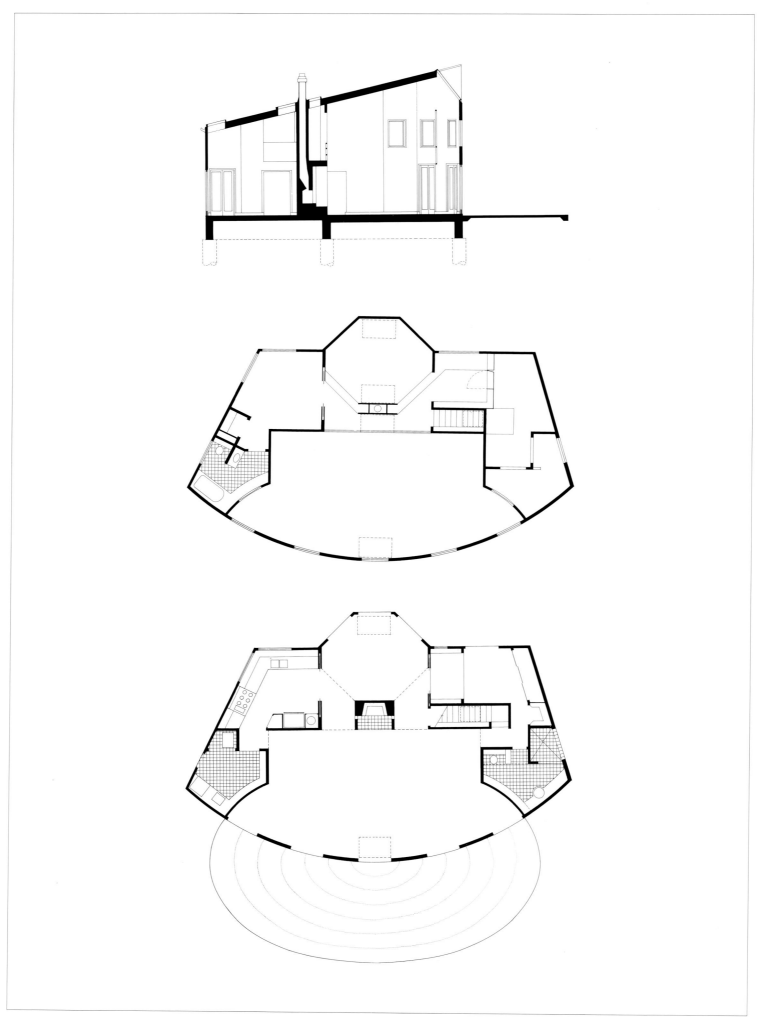

FROM ABOVE: SECTION; FIRST FLOOR PLAN; GROUND FLOOR PLAN

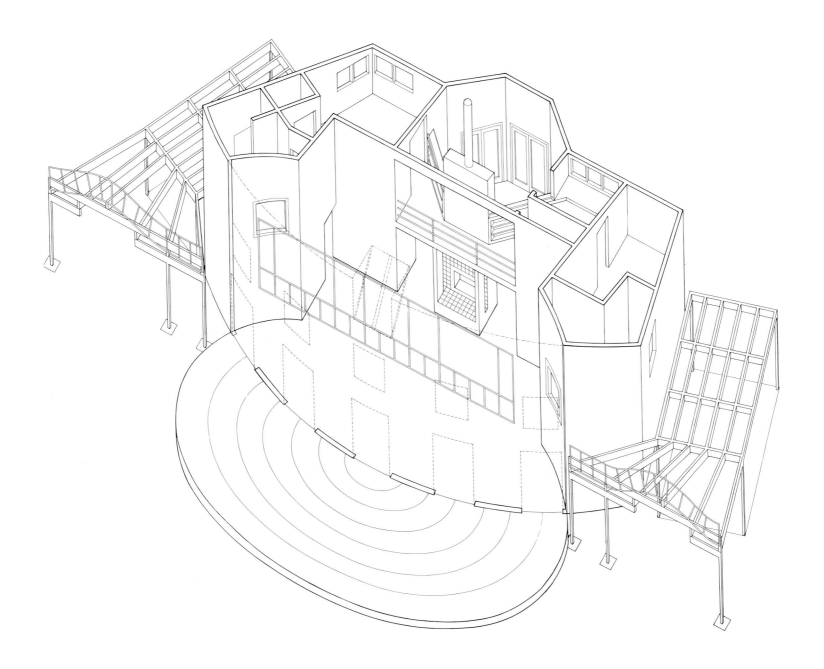

SITE PLAN

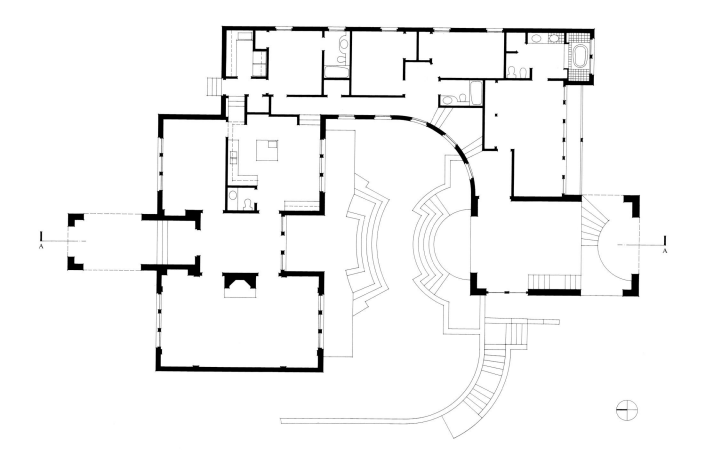

INMAN HOUSE
ATLANTA, GEORGIA

Our client's grandparents had built Atlanta's most splendid neo-baroque mansion in the 1920s, so there was some expectation that the Inmans' 2,500 square-foot house in Buckhead would evoke a formal grandness well beyond its modest size. This was aided by the site, a great piney hillside overlooking a lovely park; by the Inmans' love of Italian gardens; and by their interest in creating an outdoor porch as the main room of the house. The parti is a variation on Charles Moore's entry to the exhibition 'Houses for Sale' – an entry hall, on axis with the garden, is flanked by lofty living and dining rooms and looks downhill towards the great porch, which itself looks into the towering pines. An arc of bedrooms and their gallery link the porch to the living-dining pavilion. Cabinet shops at the Inmans' own lumber company produced triple-hung windows, mahogany doors and custom woodwork, giving special profile and detail to the carefully proportioned interiors.

Project: *Inman House*; Design Architect: *Moore Ruble Yudell*; Principal-in-charge, Principal Designer: *John Ruble*; Principal Designer: *Charles Moore*; Principal Designer: *Buzz Yudell*; *James Mary O'Connor, Peter Zingg, Brian Tichenor*

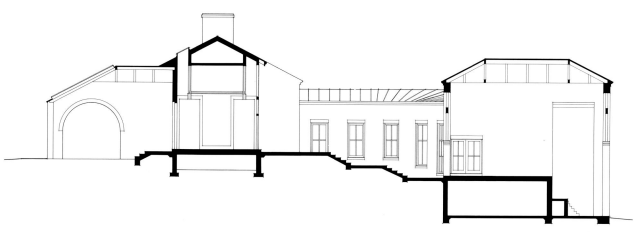

FROM ABOVE: GROUND FLOOR PLAN; LONGITUDINAL SECTION

245

FROM ABOVE: NORTH ELEVATION; SOUTH ELEVATION/SECTION; SOUTH ELEVATION; NORTH ELEVATION/SECTION

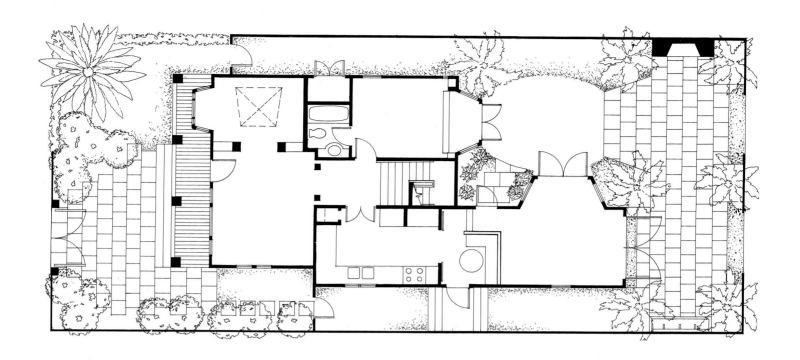

VILLA SUPERBA
VENICE, CALIFORNIA

With this expanded Venice bungalow we hoped to set a good example for a neighbourhood in which charming smaller houses are often scrapped for oversized stucco boxes. In concept, the original house is joined by a second, taller one crowned by a rooftop sleeping porch. The original bungalow is rebuilt with the same lapped siding, while its wall-house companion is scaled up with painted plywood and horizontal battens. In the front, a remodelled grander porch and glassy roof-pyramid face the street behind a shallow garden of palms and jacarandas. At the back, a walled courtyard entered through

glassy bays is lushed up by banana trees, an outdoor fireplace, and a small fountain. The superimposing of the two 'houses' and the interlocking of gardens, porches and window-bays generate inside-outside ambiguities that are continued throughout. A hallway becomes a porch for the kitchen and stairway, the upstairs bedroom has its own house-like identity, and the rooftop pavilion, a tent-like 'dach-salletl', comes and goes with the seasons.

Project: *Villa Superba;* Owner: *John Ruble;* Architect: *John Ruble;* Project Manager: *Sylvia Deily; Wendy Kohn*

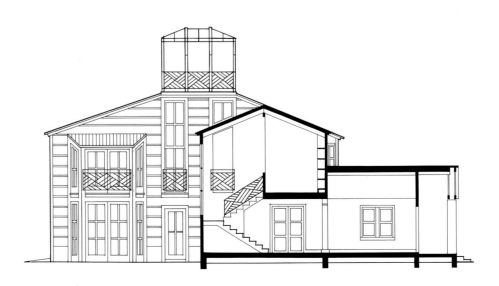

FROM ABOVE: GROUND FLOOR PLAN; NORTH ELEVATION/SECTION

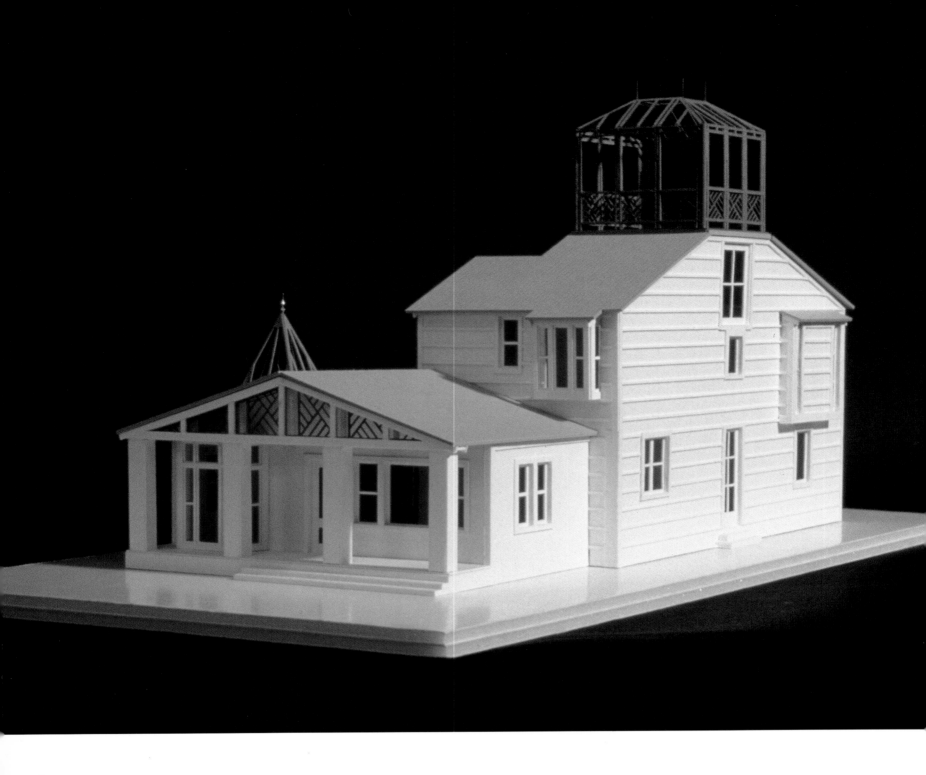

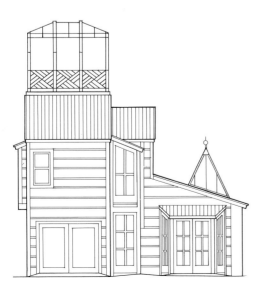

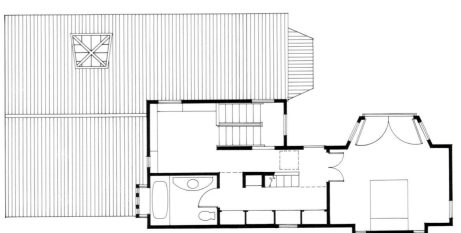

EAST ELEVATION AND SECOND FLOOR PLAN

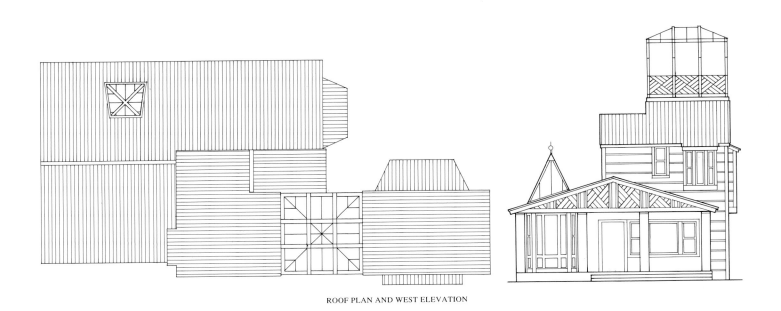

ROOF PLAN AND WEST ELEVATION

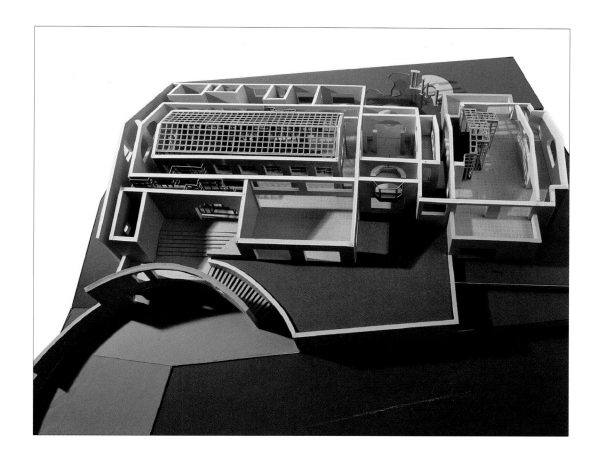

KWEE HOUSE
SINGAPORE

This is a large house, almost on the equator, built for a young Singaporean in time to receive his bride and later on, some children. For him, the library is the most important room. It lies at the heart of the house, linking in plan and section a larger courtyard and related formal rooms to a more intimate, informal courtyard and private rooms. The formal rooms – entry, living, dining, and library – surround a long courtyard garden, shaded by a dramatic overhead trellis, filled with water and lush tropical flora. The guest room, playroom, and second-floor master suite with its adjoining study overlooking the library, give onto a more intimate, informal garden court.

The site has no views, no trees, and close neighbours. Therefore, the courtyards orient the house inward for privacy and give every room generous access to the outdoors. This access is all the more important because it is really only visual, due to the unremitting equatorial heat and humidity.

The simple gabled form of the house's exterior is quietly contextual; within, a rich choreography of layered light and colour is revealed. Arcaded walls form a series of interconnected rectangles; their hues, varying subtly in value, range warmer towards the outside and cooler within. Their layering allows, simultaneously, the sense of discrete rooms and of flowing, interconnected space. Along with the overhead trellisses on the courtyards and open-work ceiling in the formal rooms, these layered walls carefully filter the strong equatorial light. The formal geometry and symmetry of architectural elements play against a more languid drift of water, tropical plants, and human movement through the house.

Project: *Kwee House;* Owner: *Liong Seen Kwee;* Design Architect: *Moore Ruble Yudell;* Principal-in-charge, Principal Designer: *Buzz Yudell;* Principal Designer: *Charles Moore;* Principal Designer: *John Ruble; Tim Felchlin, Liong Phing Kwee*

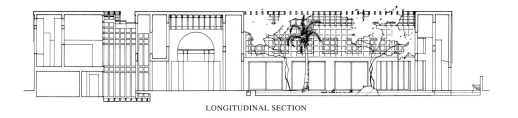

LONGITUDINAL SECTION

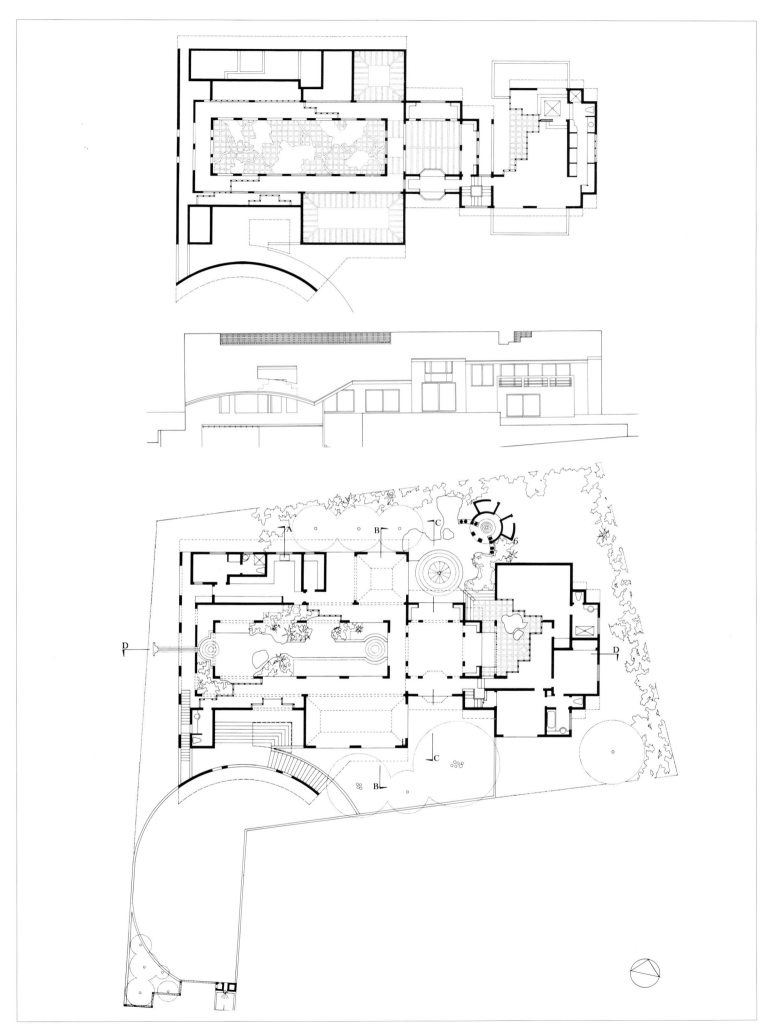

FROM ABOVE: SECOND FLOOR PLAN/REFLECTED CEILING PLAN; SOUTH ELEVATION; FIRST FLOOR PLAN/SITE PLAN

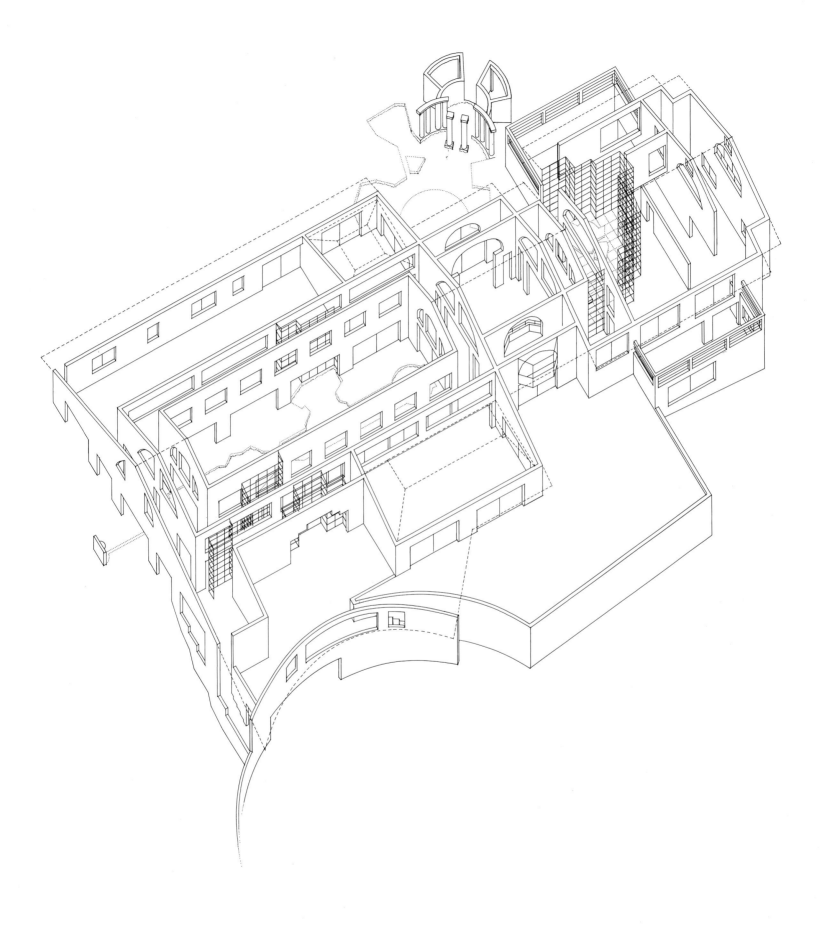

HOUSE ON POINT DUME
MALIBU, CALIFORNIA

This house, on one of the most desirable ocean-front bluffs in southern California, occupies land that has been held by the family for a long time. The owner had carefully selected views of Santa Monica, Catalina Island, the semi-private beach cove below and the lovely small canyon adjacent, that we wanted to frame within a set of walls and arcades. Between these walls, which splay out towards the sea, is a sequence of courtyards, rooms, and masses leading to a broad terrace near the edge of the cliff. Roof planes and floor lines step up in a transverse sequence from a low conservatory and children's wing, to the master bedroom that occupies a tower. The tower serves
to anchor all this movement to the bluff and provides its own terrace on top that is protected by thick parapet walls.

This house reinterprets the region's well-known Spanish idiom in a frankly modern parti, where the only ornament is colour, using tile floors, tile roofs, and smooth stucco walls.

Project: *House on Point Dume;* Design Architect: *Moore Ruble Yudell;* Principal-in-charge, Principal Designer: *Buzz Yudell;* Principal Designers: *John Ruble, Charles Moore;* Project Manager: *Daniel Garness; Akai Ming-kae Yang;* Colour: *Tina Beebe*

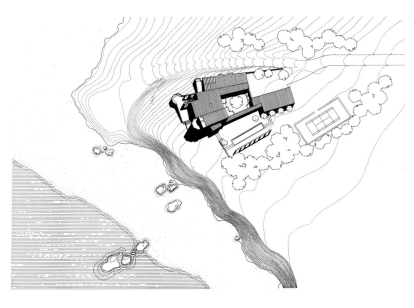

SITE PLAN

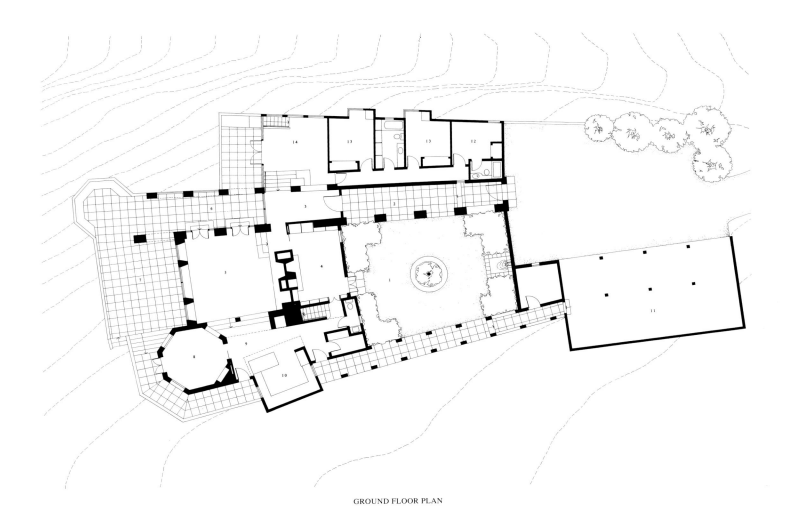

GROUND FLOOR PLAN

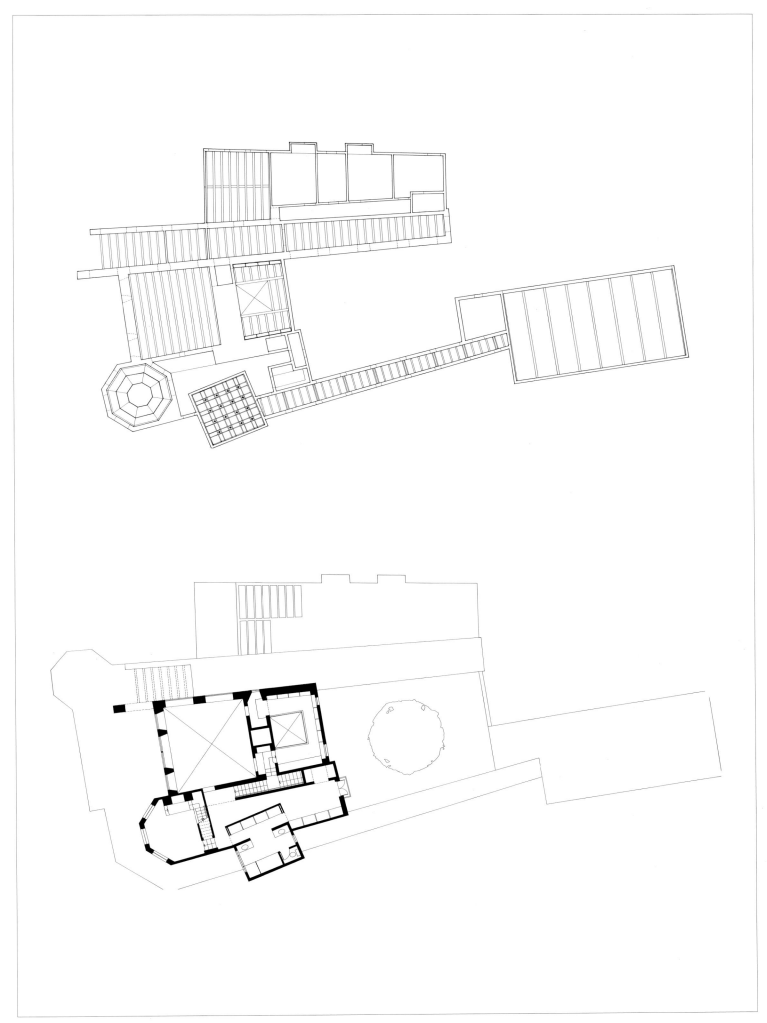

FROM ABOVE: REFLECTED CEILING PLAN; SECOND FLOOR PLAN

YUDELL/BEEBE HOUSE
MALIBU, CALIFORNIA

This house was designed by and for an architect and his wife, a graphic designer and avid gardener. Since moving to southern California they had imagined building a courtyard house in close partnership with the landscape and climate. After some years of searching, the only buildable lot in budget was a hillside lot of 100 ft x 600 ft bordered by a dry creek to its west. Coastal Commission requirements prevented building within fifty feet of this edge and Fire Department access required eighteen feet on the eastern edge. The resultant thirty-two ft x 600 ft buildable area dissuaded other buyers, but challenged and intrigued them.

The house evolved from the constraints and pleasures of the site. From east to west the house unfolds as layers of habitation: from carefully proportioned rooms to a sunny gallery broad enough for seating and dining, to a stepping street, on to a set of pergolas that function as garden rooms of varying character, then to cultivated gardens and finally to the stream-bed and uncultivated chaparral.

The north-south transformations are equally important. The lot is graced with a serene due-north mountain view and a complementary view south to the ocean. Movement along this axis connects a series of outside courtyards. One drives towards the mountain, along the eastern wall of the house, to the parking court and then begins to move through a sequence of courts heading back towards the ocean view. Inside, the gallery and library emphasise the mountain to ocean axis. Outside, the terraced street links a series of courts.

The house itself is developed in close response to concerns of proportion and light. Its extruded shape was both economical and reminiscent of farmhouses in California and other warm coastal climates. Its tower and library reach for the ocean and mountain views animating the house along its street. Despite the tight footprint, the vertical movement of the house gives every room multiple views and breezes. The hearths focus life around the warm centre of the house in winter. A sleeping porch, gallery, street, courts, and pergolas allow for connections to the benign climate and landscape for much of the year.

The richness of experience derives from the overlay of the east-west transformation (formal rooms to native landscape) with the north-south, mountain to sea movement. The interplay of geometry, space orientation and landscape creates a place that is at once serene and full of unfolding experiences.

Project: *Yudell/Beebe House;* Owner: *Buzz Yudell and Tina Beebe;* Architect: *Buzz Yudell;* Project Manager: *Akai Ming-Kae Yang;* Landscape: *Tina Beebe;* Colour: *Tina Beebe*

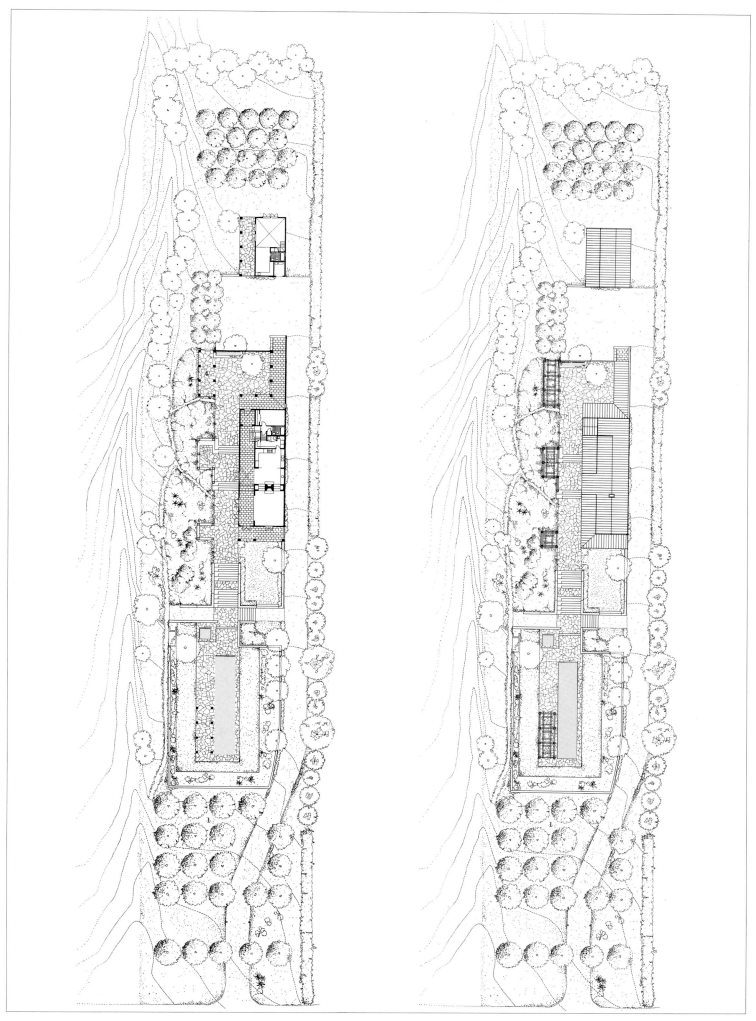

SITE PLAN AND ROOF PLAN

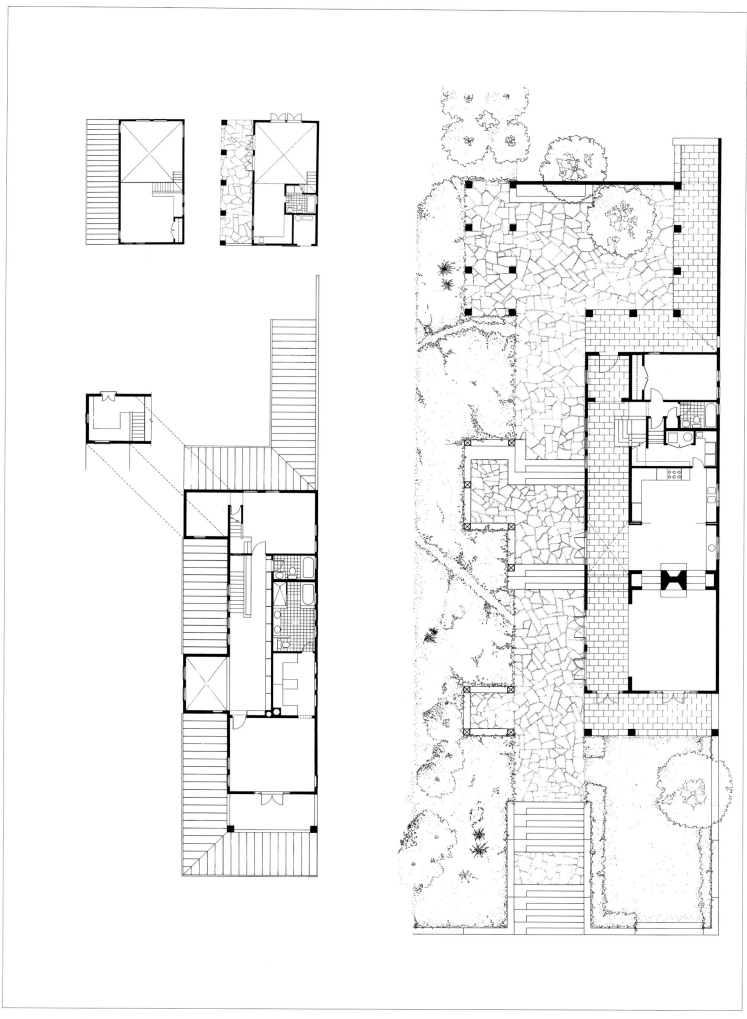

ABOVE LEFT: SECOND FLOOR PLAN AND GROUND FLOOR PLAN OF GUEST HOUSE; *BELOW LEFT:* SECOND FLOOR PLAN; *RIGHT:* GROUND FLOOR PLAN

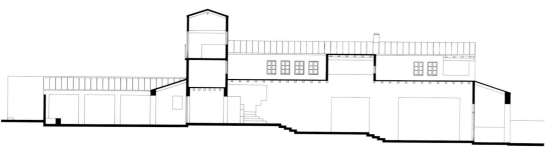

LONGITUDINAL SECTION AND CROSS SECTION

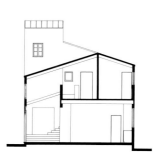

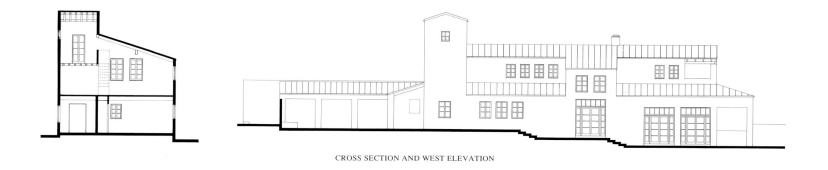

CROSS SECTION AND WEST ELEVATION

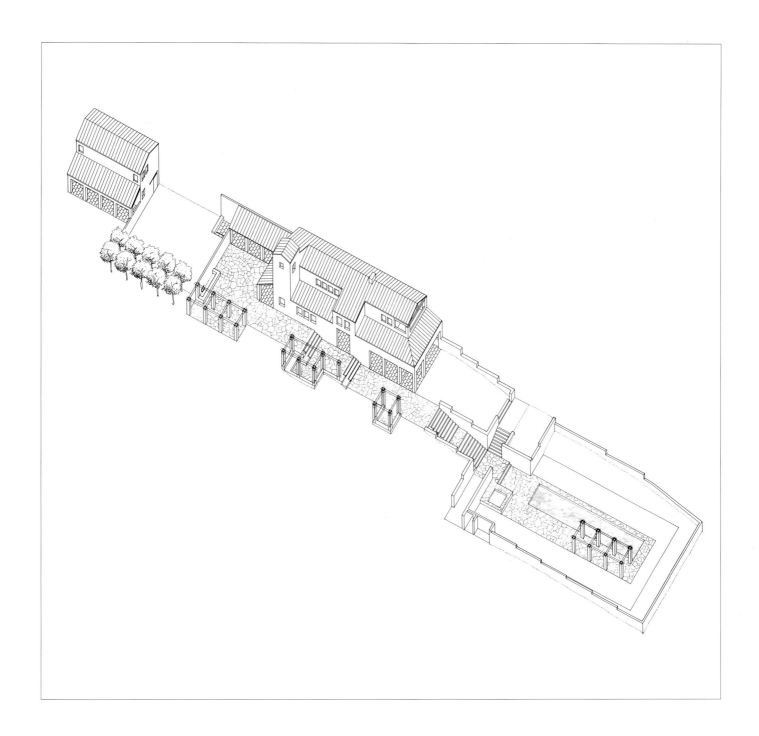

pavilion

pergola

garden room

gateway

penthouse

terrace

282

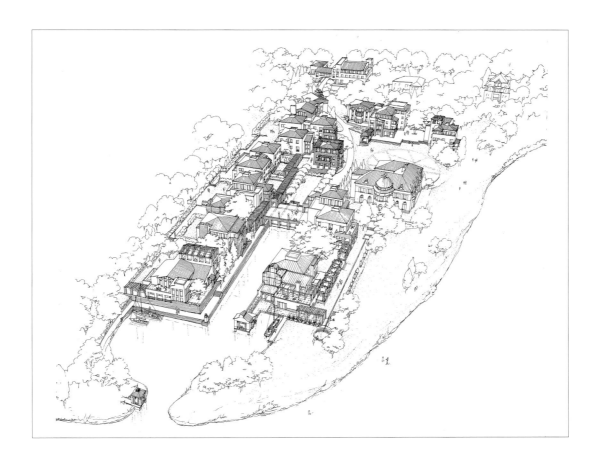

BERLINER STRASSE HOUSING
POTSDAM, GERMANY

A site for seventy-five luxury condominiums is situated south-west of Berlin at the gateway to Potsdam lying at the centre of a network of pastoral views between nineteenth-century neoclassical palaces and Baroque downtown Potsdam. An existing villa, which will be restored to late nineteenth-century splendour, stands beside the Havel River at the edge of the site. Our task was to locate twelve individual villas to complement and frame the rather large existing villa while relating to the delicate, refined scale of classical buildings by Schinkel and his colleague Persius, visible nearby. The buildings contain three-to-ten units each, and share contiguous underground parking.

The new villas, although comparable in scale to the existing house, establish a range of scales and connections to the landscape using pergolas, pavilions and roof gardens. The massing combines rational volumes and picturesque compositions, recalling memorable aspects of the 'Potsdam Style'. Traditional and simply expressive materials are used – stone bases, stucco walls and tiled roofs – adding layers of glassy towers, bays and loggias to bring the fleeting hours of sunlight deep into the units.

The site plan is divided into three distinct areas: a cluster of villas at the entry arranged around open lawns; a formal landscaped court adjacent to the existing villa, defined by arcades and symmetrical façades; and a new canal-like marina leading to the Havel River, with houses right against it to frame a dramatic view of water and park land beyond. The units are a mix of small, medium and large types which balance the formality of neoclassical plans with twentieth-century open plan interiors. A language of great rooms with bays and inglenooks creates a variety of special unit plans, while encouraging continuity in the elevations. Landscape treatment is derived from a similar idea of a set of pieces – pergolas, penthouses, and garden rooms – which connect the free-standing villas as well as recall their illustrious neighbours.

Owner: *Groth + Graalfs;* Design Architect: *Moore Ruble Yudell;* Principal-in-charge, Principal Designers: *John Ruble, Charles Moore, Buzz Yudell;* Project Manager, Designer: *Daniel Garness, C Woodhouse, M B Elliott, M Peacor, M Shoeplein, R Carvalheiro, J Taft, C Currie, D Dimster;* Landscape Architect: *Arge Müller Knippschild Wehberg;* Assoc. Architect: *Pysall Stahrenberg & Partner;* Colour: *Tina Beebe;* Project Liaison: *J Miller Stevens*

hall

bay

inglenook

porch

tower

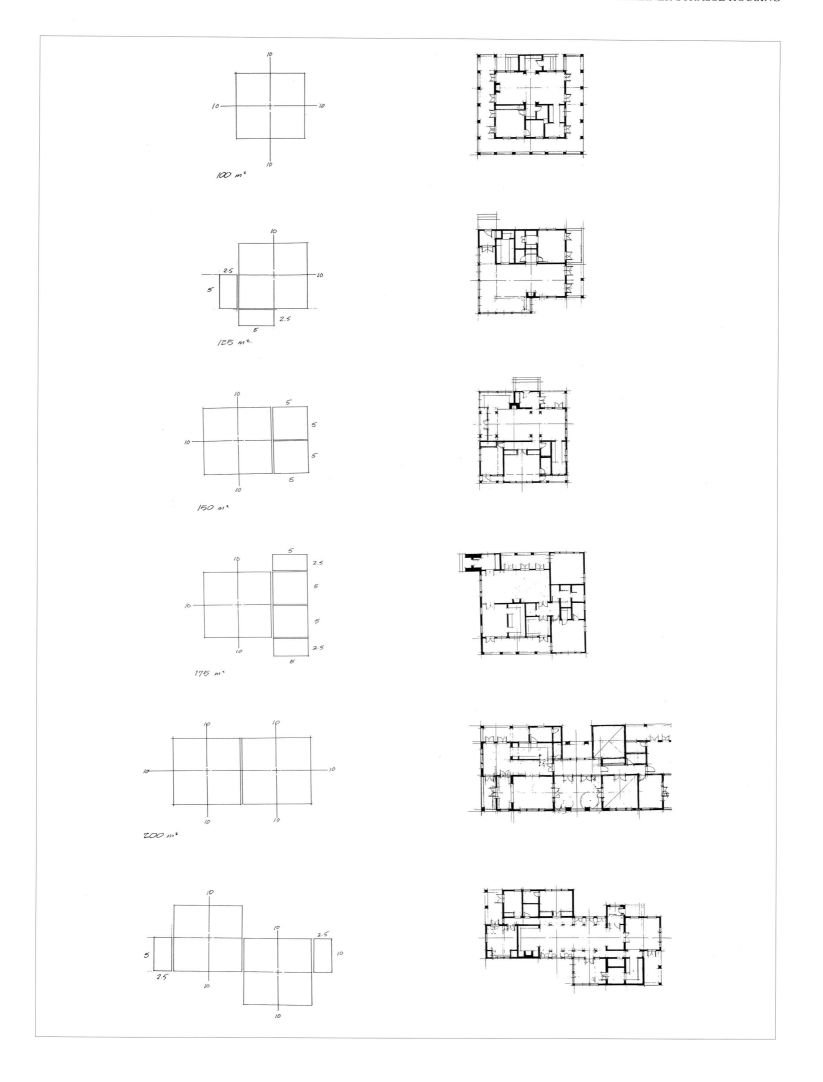

100 m²

125 m².

150 m²

175 m²

200 m²

BUZZ YUDELL

INTERVIEW BY JAMES STEELE

James Steele: How did the firm start in terms of the story behind it?

Buzz Yudell: We started as three individuals who had collaborated in various configurations and found that we enjoyed working together on an emotional level and shared sensibilities about what was important in architecture. Charles was initially a teacher/mentor and part of the shared sympathy was being influenced by this mentor and feeling a kind of a sympathetic vibration. I'm sure everybody's experienced that when you come into contact with sympathetic impulses there's a harmony that develops. All three of us had a harmony of shared sympathies, values and goals. In that sense it was the opposite of what used to be a textbook partnership out of a manual of practice, where you get one designer, one manager and one financial or PR person. Some firms work very well that way, but we started from a shared emotional and philosophical base.

JS: How did you all meet?

BY: As an undergraduate at Yale, I was aware of Charles' work. I was majoring in sculpture and taking science and humanities courses. I started sculpture in high school at about the age of fourteen and that became an extraordinarily important thing to me.

JS: Do you still have any time to do that?

BY: Occasionally I'll do little doodles out of clay but it's something I still fantasise about doing more. It's important to me within architecture, of course, but in a very different way – not strictly as a formal exercise. I was spending a lot of time with graduate sculptors in the Art and Architecture building and became very aware of what Charles was doing through this exposure and also by taking courses with Vincent Scully for whom Charles, Venturi and Kahn were quite important.

JS: What was Charles' role at that time?

BY: He started as Dean in '65 and he came in very forcefully. It was the beginning of the 60s in a sense. Charles brought with him a sense of sweeping out architecture as a kind of heroic and corporate serving endeavour, and creating a new excitement about working more directly with people and communi-

ties. He introduced a building programme in which students worked with non-profit groups designing and actually constructing buildings collaboratively. Charles' work itself was very free, expressive and inspiring. In graduate school I had Charles as a teacher in the first year. He co-taught with Kent Bloomer. They were an extraordinary duo. Kent was exuberant and warm and explored all kinds of exotic topics in geometry and philosophy. It was a very dynamic period. I became Kent's teaching assistant and then began a close friendship. In the last year of graduate school I was teaching with both of them and started to work with what was then Charles W Moore Associates – Charles' Connecticut office; which later became Moore Grover Harper and is now Centerbrook. Teaching started right out of graduate school and never stopped. That was very much under Charles' influence, too, because he brought a sense of pleasure to teaching. There was an intense communication and a sense of shared experience and exploration with the students – and that was seamless with his approach to architecture. During this period, Kent and Charles asked me to write a chapter in the *Body Memory and Architecture* book because I was studying the relationships between body movement and space in architecture. Then for a while Tina and I had our own office.

JS: In New Haven?

BY: Yes, we called it General Eclectic and we did little branch banks, interiors and small architectural jobs. In 1975, Charles was recruited by UCLA to become Programme Head. He moved to Los Angeles in keeping with his cycle of nomadic movement. We would see Charles when he came back to New Haven and he would always look excited about LA In 1976 he was becoming active with interesting new work and asked if I'd like to go to LA and work on the Rodes House and other new projects. This sounded like great fun and I'd always liked working with Charles, but thought it would be all perfect if only it were in San Francisco. I'd been to the West Coast to visit friends, usually to San Francisco, but never been to LA and suffered from the typical Easterner's prejudice about the place.

JS: What is your home town?

BY: A town called Worcester, just outside Boston. I was at school there and then Connecticut so almost all my experience except for travel was on the East Coast. I'd never thought of moving west but this seemed like an interesting adventure for a couple of years so Tina and I decided to try LA. By the time we arrived Charles was very busy with teaching and there were a lot of interesting opportunities. We began with some projects at Urban Innovations Group (the UCLA practising office), and some things just on our own.

JS: There was no office per se?

BY: Not in the first year. At first it was very informal. We worked on small houses and I helped him put together lectures. Then within a year we started realising that it would be good to have a home for what we were doing – home is almost a better word than office. Parallel with this I met John. He'd gone to the University of Virginia as an undergraduate (he'll probably tell you this in more detail) and had then gone to work for a firm in Princeton where he was working on schools. He had also worked in the Peace Corps in North Africa. After several interesting experiences, he decided to go back to graduate school to get a master's and he came to UCLA. This led to working at Urban Innovations Group on some projects with Charles. By chance, John and I found ourselves together and quickly had sympathetic feelings on a personal and artistic level. We enjoyed doing things together and soon it struck all of us that it would be great if we had an office. At first, it came out of emotion and a shared sense of purpose. It was the opposite of doing a business plan. The opposite of what you read in a textbook about how to start an office. Starting with more of an emotional motivation may give you a stronger base and a certain kind of propulsion toward the 'why' of what you're doing, as opposed to the 'how' of what you're doing.

JS: You said you started with certain sympathies in common. Could you sort of elaborate on what they are – traditional division between designer, project manager and public relations person. Has the three sort of divided into that – at all or not, in the traditional sense?

BY: I don't think it has. I'll start with the second question first. Charles, having more than one office involvement and travelling a lot, has never been very involved in running something. So that's fallen to not just John and me, but to the office as a whole entity. In that sense, Charles is in a slightly different category; although I guess we're all in the same category in that none of us 'like' the management part of it. None of us felt terribly comfortable. It was sink or swim for me and John. Suddenly, we had to go and find an accountant and a good lawyer to help us to figure out contracts. We had to do this because the office was so small at first that we couldn't afford to hire a manager. By the time we were

learning partly how to manage, we made a kind of philosophical decision: we felt that being rounded and whole and dealing with all aspects of architecture was better than having a narrow view and saying I only want to do 'X' – you take on extra burdens by saying that. We decided early on, for example, not to have a separate office manager. As we've grown, we've had to learn to get help and to delegate in many ways. At this point we have a structure that's like an executive committee in which John and I are leading or guiding but have several associate level people who are very critical to and interested in all aspects of running an office. We meet together every Monday morning and attempt to deal with all the key issues in one morning, and then various people go off with specific tasks. Mark Denton helps enormously as a kind of ombudsman for staff, hiring, scheduling, and budgeting. Stephen Harby plays a similar and central role. They both work as excellent project architects as well. Virginia Marshall does much of the financial management.

In this way, we found that we were able to avoid a traditional office manager, which for some offices works very well, but for others creates problems of the manager becoming too removed from the architecture and the staff. In similar fashion, within each individual project we have project managers who take on great management responsibility but whom we also try to see as rounded, whole people. We try to make sure that they're designing as well as managing and that they're in close design collaboration with the partners.

JS: Is there design review per se?

BY: Yes. In a way this leads back to a philosophy about how we want to live and what architecture is to us. It's important to be whole and rounded and even within a practice not to be overly specialised.

At the beginning of the office we wanted to have a few small, carefully selected projects that all three of us designed together and would follow through largely together. We had projects like St. Matthew's, the Rodes House, the Kwee house. Then in the second or third summer we did the Berlin Competition. It was an office that started with three, went to five, then to seven and so on. We all did everything and would sit down together to work. Generally, we've been able to hold on to that approach. There have been times (particularly in the last couple of years) when things might have been more frantic and suddenly we were stretched and couldn't always achieve the same degree of collaboration. As the office has grown, there have been more jobs that just two of us work on, primarily John and I in certain cases. There's a body of work that John and I will do largely together and Charles will critique and review. Then there are many jobs where three still work closely. So there may be two parallel tracks at this time.

The circle of collaboration has also broadened in

that we increasingly bring project managers and team members into the design process from the beginning. In a sense, the design review becomes not a structured process, but just a reiterative set of discussions and design sessions. We don't have a formal review process in which certain projects are pinned up and then the partners walk in and critique them. We tend to have a looser process, like a 'jam session'. This analogy of the Jazz Ensemble is something that we think about a lot because it's based on shared rhythms and melodies and a 'call and response' dialogue. One person does something, the other person responds. Somebody sketches something then there's an overlay by others. Somebody critiques, somebody else draws. Someone may be out of the loop for a while but they come back in. In the Jazz Ensemble there's improvisation but there's a lot of harmony – inevitably, there has to be or else it doesn't work. There's the chance for people to alternately put in more or less. It's a loose but harmonious structure. In a way, that analogy has really held up and it allows other people to get into the process: both associates, project managers and also, as you know, the broader participation of the office. The shared sympathies, of which I spoke before, include shared values about a way of working. This is actually quite important and it's particularly unusual for somebody older with younger partners, like Charles, that we're all pretty relaxed and not proprietary about the work. We're a contrast to the kind of firm in which three partners have three separate sets of projects.

JS: There's no ego?

BY: I won't say there's no ego, but maybe there's enough confidence for us not to feel that every piece of each project is done by every person. Rather, there's part of everybody in each project. In one project you might take it further because you suddenly had a great idea. In another, you might be uninspired that day and do less while somebody else picks up the slack. There's a sense of support about that too and the same holds with critiquing.

One shared habit is that we like to listen. We like to hear each other and we like to be criticised. We also extend that desire to listen and collaborate to our clients. We don't feel the need to have complete ownership of any one thing, yet we all feel ownership as a kind of collective, joint ownership.

You could say one set of sympathies is process-related or attitudinal and another set is based on the philosophy of what architecture can be and do. On one very simple level, architecture to all of us (and you'll probably hear us all say these things in different ways) needs to engage people in real ways that they understand. We want to communicate with people in a way that's not too removed or too abstract. We hope to engage and relate to 'places' in a similar sort of way. We look for a dialogue with a particular region or place, its history, landscape and climate so that we can weave into that fabric in some way. This is an expansion of the Jazz Ensemble analogy: the next players in it are people who inhabit the buildings and public places.

One of the most pleasurable experiences I've had (this may sound almost trite) happened as I was walking through the Crossroads School building. There was a class going on in one of the upstairs rooms that has a balcony on to the open space. They threw open the French doors and the teacher said 'Wait a second one of the students wants to talk to you'. The student came up to the balcony (I was down below in the atrium) and shouted out 'We just wanted to say we love being in this building and it's changed our lives'. That meant much more to me than having something on the cover of a magazine or any kind of award. It sounds very simple – the sense that you're giving expression to, you're creating places in which people's expression of themselves are to some extent heightened. We don't want a monologue in which you're only expressing yourself and only putting forward a set of philosophical issues in physical form, which people can learn from, but where you're not creating an invitation to participation. Places that invite people, whether on a small scale or a civic scale, to participate more actively in their environment and with one another, are fulfilling important aspects of their architectural potential. Implicitly, there's a dialogue happening in time and space. We all may talk about it slightly differently but the humanist tradition is fundamental to this approach. Later we may talk about stylistic issues. One serious concern is that the critical issues are abrogated by the labels that people have been giving to architecture. Stylistic discussions often abort discussion about cultural and social values. If our work connects to the past the emphasis is on certain archetypal connections that allow people a sense of relation to their own traditions. This is more an issue of culture, place and ethos than of style.

JS: That's an interesting point, because basically we do say that you're developing a language or looking for a language of the ways this participation can be evoked. If so, is that language a Western one, from the classical tradition? Or is there a set of signs that you come through, that you find effective in design, in a certain language of style?

BY: We're exploring how architecture can encourage and allow for this kind of social participation at various scales. In much of our work it involves studying several issues: one would be physical or typologic patterns at the building and urban scale. Sometimes it's very explicit, as in the University of Oregon where we studied the historic patterns of the campus that had been ignored and destroyed. We looked at Christopher Alexander's analysis of this campus in *The Oregon Experiment*. This was interesting because we don't see his 'pattern language' as a Bible, as many of his followers do, but there's a lot in it that overlaps with our concerns. So we found it very easy to work within that spirit although we weren't true disciples. We are constantly asking how can we relate to the place, to the land, to the way people live in that place, to the culture of the institution.

JS: Is that an intuitive thing with you or is it something that is physically structured?

BY: The intuitive part would be found in the category of sympathies. All of us would rather be about making places that people inhabit in an active participatory way, than about making places that are about architecture as a pure idea or as an abstraction. There's an intuitive part of it which is that we all feel this way. But in the last few years we've focused more on trying to find analytical tools for exploring these issues at various scales. Sometimes it's with participatory workshops. Sometimes it's the physical analysis of the patterns of places in terms of multiple scales: the scale of the house, the scale of civic realms, the scale of the city. We're now having a lot more opportunity to work at campus scale or urban scale and are able to analyse things very carefully and more methodically than we would have a few years ago. We're always searching for a balance between certain analytic approaches and the intuitive and improvisatory act.

JS: You are doing many different kinds of projects, different scales and so therefore, you don't see yourself as being trapped in one area or specialising in one area such as residential.

BY: Right. When we started the office we never thought we would do as broad a range or some of the large-scale buildings that we've done. But we always said that we wanted to be very diverse and that the excitement of architecture is in dealing with the fullness of the world, of life. The complexities and the multiple layers and agendas of different people, scales and building types stimulate our overall design process. We've always felt that it was important to work at various scales. I've been impressed that Charles has always liked working with small pieces even as his reputation and opportunities have grown. I think he may still be most comfortable with crafting a small element. In large projects he loves to focus on a few favourite parts. I know there are offices that won't do houses because it's inefficient, because they're too big an office or won't do X, Y or Z. There are certain things we wouldn't want to do, like prisons. In commercial work we only want to work with very committed developers who care deeply about urbanism. But other than that, we think of architecture as a continuum and also as a set of nesting scales that interact and feed each other. Having been involved recently with larger scale and urban projects, including analyses of housing types and patterns, I find that when we do a house, the urban design experience feeds the house experience. I wouldn't want to be laying out a piece of a city if I didn't know how to design a house, and the inverse should apply as well. Similarly, you probably wouldn't do a very good house if you didn't know how to think about designing a room or a smaller scale element. So all of those elements inform each other. When we have the choice we try to mix the scale and type of work in our office. Over the years, we've become increasingly interested in civic spaces: places between buildings and the fabric of the city. We're also getting more involved in landscape, even when we don't do the actual landscape design. We see the shaping of the spaces between buildings and relation of building to land and to inhabitants as a kind of weaving.

JS: Is there someone in the office who is specialising in landscape?

BY: Yes, we assemble a team for this when we feel it's appropriate to take on the landscape design. Tina has been getting more involved in landscape and Mario Violich, a young but very talented fellow, has a landscape degree from Berkeley. Dan Garness, who's one of our very good project architects is also fascinated by landscape. Charles, John and I, are involved at the planning and concept levels. For example, a project like Kobe Housing begins and ends with primary ideas about the way the buildings relate to the site context between the mountains and the ocean. The spaces and gardens that the building shapes are also essential to the meaning of the whole. We're now doing some houses where Tina and Mario are very involved. We still work with many landscape architects and then our buildings begin in the same way, as carefully sited responses to a particular place.

JS: You're in a city that's very difficult in terms of civic space, and that question is difficult to deal with, but how do you see that? I know Ricardo Legorreta, for example, has worked in Pershing Square, trying to incorporate some ideas from his culture. But it's a difficult problem that's facing the city, the idea of bringing people together, especially when you have so many different cultural mixes.

BY: It is a very complicated one. We have certain general goals – some of which we've been talking about – but in the end we respond by being quite specific. So, for example, the context of our project in Pasadena was that of an urbane, traditional, gridded city with major civic buildings along central axes. The original master plan had never been completed or fulfilled. A lot of the master planning (working with Larry Halprin, Barton Myers and others) involved going back to the original plan and seeing how to pick up where it left off and reinterpret it under new codes and higher density requirements. We sought to fulfil the spirit of the original

Beaux Arts plan. Also, we tried to understand the special patterns of the city. Historically, Pasadena has been a combination of very urbane, almost formal buildings complemented by a sybaritic enjoyment of gardens and open space. Pasadena has some evocation of the East Coast but is different from those cities being more of a garden city. That's in contrast with something like the master planning and 'Carousel Park' which we did at the Santa Monica Pier. The small park involved making a new entry-way, accessible ramps, children's playground, and viewing pavilions. It was a very complex little programme of bits and pieces fitting into an eccentric context. The shapes come out of the overlay of several axes of movement that occur on the site. The ramps move up as if you are boarding a boat. Railings and pavilions provide viewing of volleyball, roller skating and weight lifting. The geometries get jazzy and informal. It's beachy – you're not quite sure what's new and what's old. Each of these projects is a specific response to the place.

Playa Vista is different because it's a response to the place as a region, to Southern California as a region, and involves the development of appropriate strategies about urbanism. This was another highly collaborative effort: working with Moule-Polyzoides, Ricardo Legorreta, Duany Plater-Zyberk, Hanna/Olin and Maguire Thomas as developers.

JS: It incorporates a lot of areas doesn't it? It's so large that it crosses.

BY: It's about nine hundred acres stretching from the ocean to San Diego Freeway (about one and a half miles). It focuses on new mixed-use neighbourhoods organised by parks and streets. It has almost prototypical elements like the neighbourhood and very specific places like a marina and restored wetlands.

I guess I don't believe any of the extreme clichés about LA. I don't think, for example, that LA is all about unbridled free expression any more that most other cities. It's a little more free, a little more open and there's more sense of manifest destiny than say Boston and New York. Nor do I believe that LA is never about the pedestrian. The cliché of LA as a city of fragments without 'context' can be used as an argument to make monument buildings that are individually expressive but don't try to connect or don't try to add up to anything more cohesive. There are many places within LA where people have created local fabrics. Sometimes the fabric is linear, like Melrose Boulevard or Wilshire Boulevard; sometimes it's a piece of something like Santa Monica, Pasadena, Westwood or Hollywood. LA is energetic but not necessarily freaky or eccentric. It's fairly representative of many American cities: a complex mix of the fragments of a traditional city strung out along long axes. The axes are interconnected and are animated by multiple centres. The interaction of all this with landscape, water, mountains, desert, and gardens makes for a particularly rich place.

JS: Each one of those situations depends on what spot you're in.

BY: I don't think any of us, Charles, John or I, are people who tend towards broad theoretical pronouncements. There are things we care deeply about: issues of ethics and value. We tend to look at the situation at hand and try to think about it and about what it means to us and to the people involved. In that sense I don't think of LA as a stereotype, but as a set of potentials and complexities. There are things that make it special. The overlay of this extraordinary landscape with very complex development patterns is full of richness. It is volatile and sometimes dangerous and occasionally beautiful. The multi-centred fabric is also richly multi-cultural. It's an amazing mix and it is especially important to look at how various scales interact and diverge: what is the street corner like and the block? What's the microclimate and the microculture? These questions should be asked all the way up to the regional scale. One should look at all the nesting scales of habitation as in the Eames film, *Powers of Ten*.

JS: You're getting involved in Europe and so on and growing so much. Do you have a game plan for the future or is it just sort of happening?

BY: We don't have a game plan but we do try to have certain guiding ideas. We are growing, and what kind of a community the office should be is something we have thought a lot about; not only regarding the working process we discussed. What kind of people we have and how they relate is another question. We hire people very carefully for character and integrity as much as for all the other traditional technical and design issues. We look carefully at how we function as a group and as smaller groups on projects. We discuss how big we should be and what kind of jobs we need to keep people stimulated. I think we were almost in the mid-fifties about two years ago when things were popping in the late 80s. We found that to be a pretty difficult experience. It became more difficult to follow through on the goals I was describing.

JS: So your optimum size would be somewhere between thirty-five and fifty?

BY: Probably somewhere between twenty to forty. Once we grew over twenty we could have senior technical and management staff to support the excellent design staff that we'd always developed. We could also take on projects of any size or type. When we get much over forty to forty-five we approach our limit as partners in terms of the kind of detailed involvement we want to have. At least there's a bracket that we're starting to understand. When we remodelled this building that was borne in mind.

JS: The size of the office was basically based on the optimum size?

BY: We did a lot of looking and we were trying to balance being close to the ocean with an affordable location. We planned to move into a building that was sized for the upper end of our optimum range which would not encourage growth beyond that. If we have a 'game plan' it is only to the extent that we want to keep certain qualities of collaboration, a certain range of skills, a sense that we know everybody in the office well and that we're not fluctuating wildly. It's really a lot about the kind of community we seek.

JS: It seems like a family almost.

BY: Very much, and I think because of that and because of the way we hire, we have an extremely low turn over; some would probably say too low. I'm not saying every relationship is perfect among all members of the office, but for a lot of people much of their social and professional life revolves around the people here and what happens here. When we moved from our old space with a courtyard garden, we decided we had to have a garden because we needed this sort of outside social space which was as important as inside social spaces.

JS: When you appoint a project manager/designer for each project does that person stays with the project for the duration?

BY: Yes, from beginning to end.

JS: And then you form, you basically have a team.

BY: The ideal is to have a stable team that starts from pre-schematic or master planning and goes all the way through the design, production and construction phases. There are times when competitions occur and small jobs come and go and people have to be borrowed from one team to another. You're always having to balance the real and ideal.

JS: There are special assignment detailers.

BY: Many people do both design and technical drawings. However, a few senior technical people basically do working drawings and would not be heavily involved in the design end. Yet we try to bring them in early to critique design from their point of view. We try to have the minimum amount of specialisation that still allows us to do the best work that we can. We might take somebody who is afraid of management but who's a good designer and say 'Okay, you also have to manage this'. If somebody's timid about design we tell them they're the manager but they should also be involved in design. We gently push them into the design process. We do these things because it feels right philosophically, but I think it also makes sense in terms of the skills that people develop when they become broader in their point of view. They also enjoy it and there's more growth and satisfaction. It springs from our sense that an architect should be interested and involved in all those aspects. Architecture is the full range of these issues and one needs to understand their interrelationship. It's like multiple scales within a city. Each part informs the others.

JS: The final question concerns the order of style. You mentioned before that you're super-style – you don't think of yourself as practising with any certain style.

BY: I think that's right.

JS: I guess there have been attempts to try to push you into categories.

BY: I'm sure.

JS: You reacted very negatively – you find you don't like that idea?

BY: I find that labels do two things: they're limiting from the outside, and they can be limiting internally if you adopt them. One danger is to constrain one's own exploration and growth and the other is to limit people's perception of reality. I think labels obscure many issues in what is a search for ideas and quality that any good architect might be undertaking. The nature of the fundamental ideas and their development is so much more critical than style or fashion. For example, one of the collaborators on Playa Vista is Ricardo Legorreta who is thought of as a real modernist and we're sometimes labelled post-modernists. Well, we're not only good friends but we're very sympathetic about many things. We and Ricardo are doing parallel studies of housing and office campus projects for Playa Vista. There was more in common with the way we both approached it than there probably would have been between Ricardo and other kinds of modernists. He started off by measuring courtyards in cities he admired. He talked about proportions and scale relative to people. These were similar to our methods and concerns. We were both talking about light, climate, proportion and other elemental issues. The roof pitch might have been different. He might have had flat roofs and we might have had overhanging roofs. He might have used hot Mexican colours and we might have used a cooler palette. He might have had fewer mullions in his windows. However, in both our schemes there were strong parallels based on fundamental concerns of place and human habitation. Human actions, social interaction, connection to place and culture were common to both ways of designing. There are a set of profound, and at the same time simple, issues about what makes places not only habitable, but even ennobling. These are ancient issues of light, space, proportion, procession, experience of place and relation to its culture. Relation of place to the rituals that happen within them, and how those give voice to and ennoble the inhabitants, have to do with underlying humanist issues that one can explore exclusive of style.

We could talk about a lot of examples in our work where we ask questions about how buildings enhance human activities. At the University of Oregon the scientists emphasised the need for a 'community of scientists'. We asked how this functions and what is most important to that group of scientists in their daily life. How our physical form can support and even enlighten that process, or the lives of that group of scientists, and in turn how this building can be a citizen within its greater context. To me those issues have nothing to do with style. You see Ricardo doing that, you see Frank Gehry doing this, and Michael Graves doing the same. And these are all people that some people hate and others love. What bothers me are the people who are so extreme that they hate one kind of work and love the other without examining their fundamental intentions. I heard a well respected architect trashing Venturi on a recent jury because he 'didn't express the culture and time in which we live'. Venturi is extraordinarily thoughtful and talented, a passionate practitioner. It baffles me that anybody could get that far off to one edge to miss the profound intentions and meaning of his firm's work.

JS: One of the issues today seems to be the place of a person in architecture. If you talk to Eisenman he talks about the fact that the person has been displaced by objects and architecture should reflect that. Your viewpoint, where the person is central or people are central to the architecture, seems to be one of the key issues.

BY: It's critical, and I don't know what Eisenman would say about this but there's a kind of tripod of the building as an object, the people who inhabit it and the 'place', the physical and specific place in which it finds itself. The three interact in various ways. Maybe I should describe an episode on the Kobe project. It is illustrative of a set of underlying ideas that we care about. When we first came to the site it seemed like a place that had been damaged. It had once been a sloping site with about a seventeen metre drop across it. It was located on what had been a wonderful hillside with mountains behind and the ocean in the other direction. But it had suffered the degradations of development. It had been graded into a series of flat platforms which had south facing three-storey slabs that were called 'Danchi' which is analogous to 'dingbat' in California. It was company housing that had been dropped haplessly on these terraces. All sense of what had been the special qualities of that place were erased. So this site had

been scarred by the buildings and by a lack of anybody caring about what the site had been.

We spoke before about the building, the inhabitants and the place. We felt the need to connect to the history and character of the place and land. This is not historicism, in the sense of making buildings that look like they were there in another era – it is looking at the inherent qualities of the place; some of which may be historic, some of which have to do with the very physical characteristics. This place seemed to have lost those characteristics and yet we noticed that there were still vestiges: there was a pond in the lower part that was the result of a spring somewhere on the site which still kept on bubbling up, even though the site had been ignored and paved over. We found that this also had been a site where the water was very important for making sake – one of the most important products in that area of Kobe. So it had a wonderful history of topography, of a flow of water from a high point to a pond, of being its own hilly shape that once related to the mountains in the distance. At the same time, the city was built up all around it and it was part of the city.

Our first diagram involved the overlay of two things: an axis that related to the city, which was called the formal axis; and a path that related to nature, which we called the informal axis. The latter became a sequence of places and landscape characters commencing with a mountain garden (that was also a water source). This came through a meadow garden, crossed the city axis and then moved on to an ocean garden. On the cross axis there was a series of formal gardens: an elliptical entry, a long rectangular formal court, then the 'crossing garden' where the two geometries crossed. Finally, a white garden which was to be terminated by a chapel oriented up towards the mountains. The buildings fronted the streets in a fairly traditional way, making edges which seemed appropriate in the city. Inside, the buildings shaped the sequence of formal and informal paths and gardens. Due to the large size of the buildings, the mediation of the heights was very important and so they were stepped in ways that mediated between low and high scale elements. More importantly, the whole was a metaphor of foothills to the mountains. The buildings as foothills then shaped themselves around a valley. It was very interesting to the client because so much recent architecture there, however good, had not dealt much with landscape; even though their landscape tradition is one of the most sublime in the world.

JS: I was going to say that. I imagine you had a very sympathetic ear.

BY: We did eventually. While they liked the scheme right away, they said they were very surprised that we were trying to actually deal so much with the landscape and attempting, in a sense, to restore it. They weren't sure it was worth the effort. Then we had a wonderful moment fairly early on when, completely to our surprise, the head associated architect, Mr Misawa, came in one day with a copy of an article from a major newspaper which was written by a man named Professor Higuchi. In his thesis he wrote that the archetypal pattern of settlement in Japan was walled clusters of houses surrounding meadows with streams running through them. These ran perpendicular to the water's edge because the whole country goes from the ocean up into hills almost immediately. Typically, towns grew around streams that were perpendicular to the ocean's edge. He asserted that this was the archetypal pattern and advocated that one should build more densely, but build buildings like mountains around meadows and valleys with streams. Our Japanese associates and clients were glowing when they brought this in, for it was what we had done independently. For them, our intentions were validated by somebody who was a professor of urban geography. It made us feel good because it represented a profound way of connecting to the place.

A footnote to this relates to your question about style. This was a very complex situation because we weren't sure what we wanted to do when we began working at the site. We felt the need to relate to the place as much as we could. Yet we were not Japanese architects and didn't want to pretend that we knew all about Japanese architecture. At the same time, our clients came to us because they wanted us to do something 'Western' and they liked places such as our Berlin project. They think of American and European work as closely related – as 'Western'. Therefore, we thought, okay, we're Western architects and it's fine for us to be in the Western humanist tradition but we do desperately want the project to be about this place. The approach to the site that I just described became the most fundamental issue in that project.

As we worked on the colour, materials and detailing we tried to keep developing ideas based on the relationship to place. The buildings definitely came out of the Western classical tradition – with bases, middles and tops. Stylistically, you might think of a label but that's not really what they're about; although they come out of certain aspects of that humanist tradition. Rather, they're about making sets of places and hierarchies of experience that connect to, restore and enrich a particular place. I described this in some detail because in some ways it shows the paradoxes that we're always considering when working in another culture.

JS: That must have been quite something to deal with.

BY: Even now, I can see us doing that same project in a slightly different language – but that wouldn't change the key issues.

JS: What do you see for the future – for the office in terms of how you're going to grow, and in terms of where you're headed?

BY: That's a good question.

JS: What would you like to see happen to the office?

BY: We'd like to do largely what we're currently doing but with perhaps a little more exploration of qualities of material and construction. It's something we've started to do more. A lot of early work was small and on very modest budgets – not that what we're doing is necessarily on expensive budgets. But I think in the last few years we've been a little more exploratory about material.

JS: You've also had developers as clients.

BY: Yes, which can be very challenging. So thinking about the expressive potential of different materials may sound like a detail, but it's important. Another area that we find stimulating is urban design. It feeds back into the individual buildings. We're starting to have more opportunities such as Playa Vista in Los Angeles. We're also working in Europe at an urban scale. Recently, we've been collaborating with Rob Krier, Burelli and others on a master plan for a new town at Kirchsteigfeld, a district of Potsdam. This is especially interesting to us. Another thing that we have been doing for a while – which may relate to some of these stylistic questions – is exploring expression: how the range of expression overlays with the fundamental issues of place and habitation. What happens if we detail things more abstractly? Do we lose some of these qualities or do we gain something else? What is the range of expression within the principles we hold as fundamental?

JS: It seems as though you really have a leeway to find out where that is.

BY: Yes, exactly. But I don't think the fundamentals are going to change for us. One thing we have found increasingly important is greater involvement in landscape as it relates to the buildings. We're still working with landscape architects but we're thinking more about and taking more initiatives on those interactions. In another area (and maybe these all relate), we feel, as an office, a real hungering for a broader involvement in the community in terms of civic issues and housing. This goes way back to Charles' commitments in the early 60s to do low cost public housing and to become involved in nonprofit and self-help projects through the university. Having been students in that era and experienced the satisfaction of such involvements, one doesn't, I think, lose the need for civic and social meaning in architecture. We're able to be involved to the extent that we're doing civic projects and university projects. At the moment, we're only able to do public housing in other countries; like in Sweden where we're doing 'social' housing, and in Germany where the Kirchsteigfeld plan is based on a public-private partnership for affordable housing.

JS: Which project is that?

BY: It's a planning project in a part of Potsdam for a client named Groth & Graalfs. We're also doing villas on the Berliner Strasse in the fancier part of Potsdam for the same clients. The latter project uses the villa prototype modified to house multiple flats in a beautiful historic part of Potsdam. The planning project, in an area called Kirchsteigfeld, involved three German architects: Eyl & Partners, Nielebock & Partners, Krüger & Partners; plus Rob Krier, the Italian architect named Burelli, and us. We were all asked to do schemes and had a two-phased process in which we did individual schemes first. Then we held a workshop to critique and consolidate ideas. The master plan is going to synthesise schemes by Krier and us. All six firms will do parts of the housing. It's going to be about seventy-five percent social housing. The public realm is also given a great deal of importance with the integration of parks, squares, landscape, schools and other civic buildings within neighbourhoods.

I guess you can see that we're increasingly interested in urban issues, civic issues, housing and exploring more about building to landscape relationships. The stylistic issue is not first in that hierarchy. One of the reasons we don't want labels is that we certainly want the freedom to explore and to evolve formally and aesthetically. I've been exploring and finding it satisfying to pursue forms and orders that are more serene and more understated than I might have wanted to a few years ago. Working on my own house with Tina and thinking about how we wanted to live, crystallised a lot of issues about places that I've felt good in, which had to do with materials, proportion, light, space and connection with the landscape – many of the things we've been talking about. I've been finding this process of becoming calmer, quieter and more serene, while relating to the underlying issues, to be very gratifying, even if it doesn't make flashy objects. We all want to have the freedom to experiment and explore a range but I don't think any of us are interested in jumping onto a certain bandwagon of the moment. We're not about to put on constructivist clothing.

JS: I think the direction you're taking certainly has a level of longevity to it.

BY: I would hope that in ten or twenty years from now we would feel as committed to what we're doing as we have for the last fifteen years. We look back at the Rodes house, which when it was built and published was highly regarded, but was called everything from post-modern, to post modern classicism or even a new modernism. We still feel it's a house that deals with both abstractions and connections to place and time. It has references to the archetypal house and also fresh interpretations of how spaces are used. I think that's been true of the Kwee house in other ways. It develops formal geometries along axes to create both traditionally defined rooms and courts. It creates a place responsive to the light and climate of the near equatorial site. But it also creates surprise by the complex interpenetration and unfolding of spaces. Our house takes simple geometries and layer them on an agrarian site to create a quiet complexity of experiences. Shaping places for habitation and connections to the land takes precedence over expression of the object alone. Some of our projects become more specific because of where they're situated, like Pasadena and Berlin. Working in these areas, we may have more historical connection. I would hope to see more dialogue about the issues we've been talking about and a little cooling down of concern with fashion. Do you think that might happen or . . .

JS: I think journalists tend to label things because it's the way to generate interest.

BY: They have to find the new thing or help stimulate it.

JS: I think people are yearning for architecture that is stable.

BIOGRAPHIES

CHARLES W MOORE

Charles Moore has received international acclaim as an architect, writer and teacher. His ability to capture the essential character of the places where be builds, embodying a respect for the past in contemporary forms, is a reflection of his own broad experience. Educated in the Midwest (Michigan, BArch) and in the East (Princeton, PhD), he began his award-winning work in Northern California, where a series of houses, and the Sea Ranch Condominiums in particular, attracted national attention and profoundly influenced the course of contemporary practice. He served as the chairman of the architecture department at Berkeley while remaining actively involved with the firm of Moore Lyndon Turnbull Whitaker.

In 1965, he moved east to become the dean of the School of Architecture at Yale, an association that was to last ten years. During that time he developed his ideas and concerns in a series of books, *The Place of Houses*, *Dimensions*, and *Body, Memory and Architecture*. He continued to build, through Moore Lyndon Turnbull Whitaker/Moore Turnbull, and later the firm Moore Grover Harper, with influential residential work now accompanied by larger projects of public housing and campus planning. His work in these areas set new standards for imaginative and humane design within the difficult constraints of public funding and regulations.

In 1975, an appointment to the UCLA School of Architecture and Planning brought Charles Moore back to California where his career had begun. With the establishment of the Los Angeles office of Moore Ruble Yudell in 1977, Moore's practice began to involve projects of increased scope and complexity, while he developed with his partners a unique expertise in community involvement and participatory design. An undiminished enthusiasm for houses and housing is joined by opportunities that include waterfronts, world fairs, art institutions and civic centres. As his work has grown in variety and scale, Charles Moore has retained his deep concerns for the historical, architectural and natural features of the places where he is asked to build, fusing this sense of place with a noted sensitivity to the dreams and aspirations of his clients.

Education

Princeton University, doctor of philosophy, 1957
Princeton University, master of fine arts in architecture, 1956
University of Michigan, bachelor of architecture, 1947

Teaching Experience

O'Neill Ford Professor of architecture, School of Architecture, University of Texas, Austin, 1985–
Professor, University of California, Los Angeles,
School of Architecture and Urban Planning, 1984 to present
Professor, Yale University School of Architecture, 1970 to 1975
Dean, Yale University School of Architecture, 1965 to 1970
Associate Professor, Chairman, University of California, Berkeley, department of architecture, 1959 to 1965
Associate Professor, Princeton University School of Architecture, 1957 to 1959
Assistant Professor of architecture, University of Utah, 1950 to 1952

Professional Experience

Principal, Moore Ruble Yudell, Santa Monica, California, 1977 to present
Principal, Moore Grover Harper/Centerbrook, Essex, Connecticut, 1974 to present
Associated with Urban Innovations Group (practice arm of UCLA School of Architecture), 1975 to present
Principal, Charles W Moore Associates, Essex, Connecticut, 1970 to 1974
Principal, MLTW/Moore Turnbull, San Francisco, California, 1965 to 1970
Principal, Moore Lyndon Turnbull Whitaker (MLTW), 1962 to 1964
Clark and Beuttler, San Francisco, California, 1959 to 1962
Lieutenant, US Army Corps of Engineers in the United States, Japan and Korea, 1952 to 1954
Worked in offices of Mario Corbett, Joseph Allen Stein, and Clark and Beuttler, San Francisco, California, 1947 to 1949

Awards & Distinctions

American Institute of Architects, Gold Medal for a lifetime of professional achievement, 1991
American Institute of Architects, Twenty-five Year Award, 1991 – Sea Ranch Condominiums
American Wood Council, Honour Award, 1991 – First Church of Christ, Scientist
Los Angeles Chapter, American Institute of Architects, Honour Award, 1989 – Humboldt Library
California Council, American Institute of Architects, Merit Award, 1989 – Anawalt House
American Institute of Architects Honour Award, 1988 – Tegel Harbour Housing
California Council, American Institute of Architects, Honour Award, 1988 – Tegel Harbour Housing
American Institute of Architects Honour Award, 1987 – Hood Museum of Art
First Prize, City of Oceanside Civic Center Competition, 1986
American Institute of Architects Honour Award, 1984 – St Matthew's Church
California Council, American Institute of Architects, Merit Award, 1984 – St Matthew's Church
Los Angeles Chapter, American Institute of Architects, Merit Award, 1984 – St Matthew's Church
First Prize, Beverly Hills Civic Center Competition, 1982
Architectural Record Houses of the Year, 1981 – Rodes House
First Prize, Tegel Harbour International Design Competition, West Berlin 1980 – Housing, Recreational and Cultural Center
Progressive Architecture Citation, 1977 – Riverdesign Dayton
AIA-HUD Award, 1970 – Public Housing, Middletown, Connecticut
New England Region American Institute of Architects Honour Award, 1970 – Klotz House
Progressive Architecture Citation, 1970 – Santa Cruz College No 6 (Kresge College)
Progressive Architecture, First Honour Award, 1970 – Pembroke Dormitory
Architectural Record Award of Excellence, 1970, Naff House
HUD Award, 1969 – Church Street South
Architectural Record Award of Excellence, 1969 – McElrath House
Fellow, American Institute of Architects, 1968
AIA/*Sunset* Award of Merit, 1968 – Lawrence House
AIA/*Sunset* Award of Merit, 1967 – Johnson House
Bay Area American Institute of Architects Award of Merit, 1967 – Sea Ranch Swim Club
American Institute of Architects Honour Award, 1967 – Sea Ranch Condominiums
Progressive Architecture Citation, 1966 – Sea Ranch Swim Club
California Governor's Design Award, 1966 – Sea Ranch Condominiums
Progressive Architecture Citation, 1965 – Sea Ranch Condominiums
American Institute of Architects Honour Award, 1965 – Citizens Federal Savings and Loan (with Clark and Beuttler)
Progressive Architecture Citation, 1964 – Jewell House
AIA/*Sunset* Special Award, 1963-64 – Bonham House
AIA/*House and Home* First Honour Award, 1963 – Jobson House
Progressive Architecture Citation, 1963 – Coronado Condominium
Progressive Architecture Citation, 1962 – Moore House
Architectural Record Award of Excellence, 1962 – Hubbard House
AIA/*Sunset* Award, 1961-62 – Hubbard House

Published Books

The Poetics of Gardens, with William J Mitchell and William Turnbull, Jr, MIT Press, 1988
The City Observed: Los Angeles, with Peter Becker and Regula Campbell, Vintage Press, 1984
Body, Memory and Architecture, with Kent Bloomer and Robert Yudell, Yale University Press, 1977
Dimensions, with Gerald Allen, McGraw/Hill, Architectural Record Books, 1976
The Place of Houses with Gerald Allen and Donlyn Lyndon, Holt Rinehart Winston, 1974

Selected Work

Cultural Center, Escondido, California, in progress
Sundsterrassen Housing, Malmo, Sweden, in progress
Kobe Nishiokamoto Housing, Kobe, Japan, in progress
School of Business Administration, University of California, Berkeley, in progress
Beverly Hills Civic Center: Police Station and Library, Beverly Hills, California, 1991
Plaza Las Fuentes mixed-use development, Pasadena, California, 1989
Humboldt Library, Berlin, West Germany, 1989
San Antonio Art Institute, San Antonio, Texas, 1988
Tegel Harbour Housing, Berlin, West Germany, 1987
Tegel Harbour Master Plan, Berlin, West Germany, 1980 – present
Beverly Hills Civic Center: Fire Station, Beverly Hills, California, 1987
Beverly Hills Civic Center: Parking Garage, Beverly Hills, California, 1985
Hood Art Museum, Dartmouth College, 1985
Louisiana World Exposition Site Planning and Theme Buildings, New Orleans, 1984
St Matthew's Church, Pacific, Palisades, California, 1983
Sweetwater Country Club and Resort Condominiums, Houston, Texas, 1983
Residence, Aspen, Colorado, 1980
'Roanoke Design 79', Roanoke, Virginia, 1979
Restoration Plan, Seal Beach, California, 1979 (project)
Rodes Residence, Los Angeles, California, 1979
St Joseph's Fountain, New Orleans, Louisiana, 1978
Residence, Ojal, California, 1978
'Riverdesign', Dayton, Ohio, 1976
Gund House, Princeton, New Jersey, 1975
Xanadune Resort Development, St Simon's Island, Georgia, 1972 (project)
Maplewood Terrace Low-Income Housing, Middletown, Connecticut, 1971
Kresge College, University of California, Santa Cruz, 1970
Budge House, Heraldsburg, California, 1966
Sea Ranch Condominiums, Sea Ranch, California, 1965
Moore House, Orinda, California, 1962
Jobson House, Palo Colorado Canyon, California, 1961

JOHN RUBLE

John Ruble began his career in architecture and planning in 1970 by working as a volunteer town planner in North Africa. Out of that experience grew a number of special interests that continue to guide his work: an awareness of architecture as response to site and climate, and a commitment to the participation of client and community in design. He worked as designer for Uniplan, in Princeton, winning AIA awards for a number of institutional and urban projects. Moving to Los Angeles in 1974, he completed a graduate degree at UCLA, where he began his association with Charles Moore on an urban design study for Marburg, Germany, and on a number of residential works.

With the establishment of Moore Ruble Yudell in 1977, John Ruble joined Moore and Yudell in collaboration on a wide range of work, including planning for coastal areas in California and design for commercial and institutional projects of increasingly larger scale. His involvement as principal-in-charge includes St Matthew's Church; Tegel Harbour in Berlin; Carousel Park at the Santa Monica Pier; and the Molecular Biology Research Facility Unit II, University of California, San Diego, for the Howard Hughes Medical Institute.

Education

University of California, Los Angeles, School of Architecture and Urban-Planning, master of architecture, 1976
University of Virginia, bachelor of architecture, 1969

Teaching Experience

Lecturer, University of California, Los Angeles, School of Architecture and Urban Planning, 1981 to 1986
Visiting Lecturer, Cornell University, 1976
Teaching Associate, University of California, Los Angeles, School of Architecture and Urban Planning, 1975

Professional Experience

Principal, Moore Ruble Yudell, Santa Monica, California, 1977 to present
Consultant, Direct Energy Corporation, Irvine, California (solar heating and cooling development grant, US Department of Energy), 1977 to 1978
Associated with Charles W Moore, Los Angeles, 1976 to 1977
Project Manager, Urban Innovations Group, Los Angeles, 1976 to 1977
Associated with OM Ungers, Ithaca, New York, 1976
Designer, Uniplan, Princeton, New Jersey, 1971 to 1975
Urban Designer, Peace Corps, Tunisia Kasserine Bureau d'Urbanisme, Ministère de Tourisme et Aménagement du Territoire, 1969 to 1970

Selected Published Work

'Moore Ruble Yudell – A Malibu Residence', *Architectural Digest*, February 1990 – House on Point Dume
'Pride of Place', *Architectural Record*, January 1990 – Humboldt Library
'Waterfront Housing at Once Exuberant and Classical', *Architecture*, May 1988 – Tegel Harbour Housing
'Berlin 1988', *Abitare*, May 1988, Milano, Italy – Tegel Harbour
'Housing That's Changing the Face of West Berlin', *The New York Times*, April 14, 1988 – Tegel Harbour
'Living by the Water', (cover), *Progressive Architecture*, October 1987 – Tegel Harbour Housing
'Moore Ruble Yudell – Remodelling a Spanish Colonial House in Beverly Hills' (cover), *Architectural Digest*, September 1987 – Pynoos House
'Charles Moore' (cover), *Interiors*, September 1987 – St Matthew's Church, Church of the Nativity, Humboldt Library
'Rebuilding Berlin – Yet Again', *Time*, June 15, 1987 – Tegel Harbour Housing
'Das Pathos endet an der Haustür', *Der Spiegel*, June 1, 1987 – Tegel Harbour Housing
Charles Moore, Buildings and Projects 1949-1986, Eugene J Johnson, ed New York, *Rizzoli*, 1986 – St Matthew's Church, Tegel Harbour Housing, Humboldt Library, San Juan Capistrano Library
'Overview of Recent Works', *Space Design*, November 1986 – Tegel Harbour, Plaza Las Fuentes, The Parador Hotel, St Matthew's Church, San Antonio Art Institute, Kwee House
'Architecture – Moore Ruble Yudell', *Architectural Digest*, August 1985 – Kwee House
'Built on Religious, Regional Tradition, St Matthew's Church', *Architecture*, May 1984, Washington DC
'Design by Congregation', *Architectural Record*, February 1984 – St Matthew's Church
'St. Matthew's Parish Church', *Architecture + Urbanism*, January 1984, Tokyo 1981
Erste Projekte, *Internationale Bauausstellung Berlin 1984*, West Berlin 1981 – Tegel Harbour
'A Church is Not a Home', *Newsweek*, March 1983 – St Matthew's Church
'Charles Moore: Recent Projects', *Architectural Review*, August 1981, London
'Houses of the Year', *Architectural Record*, May 1981 – Rodes House
'New American Architecture 1981', *Architecture + Urbanism*, 1981, Tokyo
'Charles Moore and Company', *Global Architecture No 7*, Tokyo 1980

Selected Awards, Distinctions & Exhibits

Los Angeles Chapter, American Institute of Architects, Honour Award, 1989 – Humboldt Library
American Institute of Architects Honour Award, 1988 – Tegel Harbour Housing
California Council, American Institute of Architects, Honour Award, 1988 – Tegel Harbour Housing
California Council, American Institute of Architects, Honour Award, 1988 – Carousel Park, Santa Monica Pier
Building a Better Future Honour Award, 1987 (State of California Department of Rehabilitation Architectural Design Awards Programme) – Carousel Park
City of Santa Monica Mayor's Commendation, October 1987 – Carousel Park
Excellence on the Waterfront Honour Award, Waterfront Center, 1987 – Carousel Park
'Der Revision der Moderne Postmodern, Architecture 1960-1980', Deutsches Architekturmuseum, Frankfurt, West Germany, 1984
'Das Abenteuer der Ideen', National Galerie, Berlin, West Germany, 1984
American Institute of Architects Honour Award, 1984 – St Matthew's Church
California Council, American Institute of Architects, Merit Award, 1984 – St Matthew's Church
Los Angeles Chapter, American Institute of Architects, Merit Award, 1984 – St Matthew's Church
'Contemporary Views of the House', Mandeville Gallery, University of California San Diego, 1983
'The California Condition', La Jolla Museum of Contemporary Art, 1982
'Houses and Cities', Bernard Jacobson Gallery, Los Angeles, 1982
First Prize, Santa Monica Pier Design Charrette, 1981
First Prize, Tegel Harbour International Design Competition, West Berlin 1980 – Housing, Recreational and Cultural Center
St Matthew's Parish Church, Exhibition, Max Protech Gallery, New York City, 1980
'LA by LA', Exhibition 1980 – Kwee House
'Late Entries to the Tribune Competition', drawing exhibited in Centre Pompidou, Paris, St Louis Art Museum, Museum of Contemporary Art Chicago, 1979-1980

New Jersey Society of Architects Citation, 1974 – Marlboro Middle School (with Uniplan)
New Jersey Society of Architects Citation, 1973 – East Orange Middle School (with Uniplan)

Selected Work
Escondido Cultural Center, Escondido, California, in progress
Sundsterrassen Housing, Malmö, Sweden, in progress
University of Washington Chemistry Building, Seattle, Washington, in progress
Malibu House, Malibu, California, in progress
School of Business Administration, University of California, Berkeley, in progress
Boxenbaum Arts Education Centre, Crossroads School, Santa Monica, California, 1989
Howard Hughes Medical Institute/Molecular Biology Research Facility II, UC San Diego, California, 1989
Humboldt Library, Berlin, West Germany, 1989
Tegel Harbour Housing, Berlin, West Germany, 1987
Tegel Harbour Master Plan and Promenade, Berlin, West Germany, 1980 to present
Inman House, Atlanta, Georgia, 1986
Ocean Park Master Plan and Beach Improvements, Santa Monica, California, 1986
Carousel Park, Santa Monica Pier, Santa Monica, California, 1986
St Matthew's Church, Pacific Palisades, California, 1983
Santa Monica Pier Master Plan and Design Guidelines, Santa Monica, California, 1982
Fourth Federal Design Assembly Lounges, Washington DC, 1978
City Hall, Long Branch, New Jersey, with Uniplan, 1973
High School, Pemberton, New Jersey, with Jules Gregory, 1973
Kasserine General Plan, Tunisia, with Kasserine Bureau d'Urbanisme, 1970

BUZZ YUDELL
Buzz Yudell, AIA, has been active in both architectural practice and education since his graduation from the Yale School of Architecture in 1972. He has collaborated extensively with Charles W Moore: first as a project manager in Moore's Connecticut office, then as a co-teacher at Yale, and since 1977 as a principal in Moore Ruble Yudell. As a professor at UCLA, teaching and writing have remained important priorities, and his interest in community issues led to involvement in a number of participatory planning projects. More recently he has been principal-in-charge for major building projects, including four new science buildings for the University of Oregon, which included a series of intensive user workshops in the design process; Plaza Las Fuentes, a six-acre mixed-use development in the historic centre of Pasadena; the renovation of UCLA's historic Powell Library; the Escondido Cultural Center; Nishiokamoto Housing in Kobe, Japan; and master planning for Playa Vista, a 900 acre mixed-use community in Los Angeles.

Education
Yale School of Architecture, master of architecture, 1972
Yale College, bachelor of arts *cum laude*, 1969

Teaching Experience
Adjunct Professor, University of California, Los Angeles, School of Architecture and Urban Planning, 1977 to present
Visiting Critic, Technical University of Nova Scotia, Halifax School of Architecture, 1983
Visiting Critic, University of Texas at Austin School of Architecture, 1981
Visiting Critic in Architectural Design, Yale School of Architecture, 1971 to 1976

Selected Published Writing
'Collisions of the Ideal and the Uncertain', *Space Design* No 266, November, 1986
'Moore in Progress', *Global Architecture* No 7, Tokyo, 1980
Body, Memory and Architecture, contributor with Charles W Moore and Kent Bloomer, 1977
'Architecture 1976', with Charles W Moore, Funk & Wagnalls 1976 *Encyclopedia Yearbook*, New York
'Architecture 1973', with Charles W Moore, Funk & Wagnalls 1973 *Encyclopedia Yearbook*, New York

Selected Published Work
'Moore Ruble Yudell – A Malibu Residence', *Architectural Digest*, February 1990 – House on Point Dume
'Pride of Place', *Architectural Record*, January 1990 – Humboldt Library
'Waterfront Housing at Once Exuberant and Classical', *Architecture*, May 1988 – Tegel Harbour Housing
'Berlin 1988', *Abitare*, May 1988, Milano, Italy – Tegel Harbour
'Housing That's Changing the Face of West Berlin', *The New York Times*, April 14, 1988 – Tegel Harbour
'Living by the Water'(cover), *Progressive Architecture,* October 1987 – Tegel Harbour Housing
'Moore Ruble Yudell – Remodeling a Spanish Colonial House in Beverly Hills'(cover), *Architectural Digest*, September 1987 – Pynoos House
'Charles Moore' (cover), *Interiors,* September 1987 – St Matthew's Church, Church of the Nativity, Humboldt Library
'Rebuilding Berlin – Yet Again', *Time*, June 15, 1987 – Tegel Harbour Housing
American Houses, Philip Langdon, New York: Stewart, Talbori & Chang, 1987 – King Studio, Marine Street Residence
'Perfection in Miniature', *House Beautiful*, February 1987 – King Studio
Freestyle, Tim Street-Porter, New York: Stewart, Tabori & Chang, 1986 – Rodes House, Marine Street Residence
Charles Moore, Buildings and Projects 1949-1986, Eugene J Johnson, ed, New York: Rizzoli, 1986 – St Matthew's Church, Tegel Harbour Housing, Humboldt Library, San Juan Capistrano Library
'Overview of Recent Works', *Space Design*, November 1986 – Tegel Harbour, Plaza Las Fuentes, The Parador Hotel, St Matthew's Church, San Antonio Art Institute, Kwee House
Erste Projekte, Internationale Bauausstellung Berlin 1984, West Berlin 1981 – Tegel Harbour
'A Church is Not a Home', *Newsweek*, March 1983 – St Matthew's Church
'Charles Moore: Recent Projects', *Architectural Review*, August 1981, London
'Back to the Classics', *Newsweek*, September 1981, New York – Rodes House
'Houses of the Year', *Architectural Record*, May 1981 – Rodes House
'New American Architecture 1981', *Architecture and Urbanism*, 1981, Tokyo

'Palladio Lives On', *Life Magazine*, 1980, New York – Rodes House
'Charles Moore and Company', *Global Architecture* No 7, Tokyo 1980

Selected Awards, Distinctions & Exhibits
American Wood Council, Honour Award, 1991 – First Church of Christ, Scientist, Glendale, California
California Council, American Institute of Architects, Honor Award, 1991 – First Church of Christ, Scientist, Glendale, California
American Institute of Architects/American Library Council Award, 1990 – Humboldt Library
Los Angeles Chapter, American Institute of Architects, Honour Award, 1990 – Humboldt Library
California Council, American Institute of Architects, Merit Award, 1989 – House on Point Dume
American Institute of Architects Honour Award, 1988 – Tegel Harbour Housing
California Council, American Institute of Architects, Honour Award, 1988 – Tegel Harbour Housing
California Council, American Institute of Architects, Honour Award, 1988 – Carousel Park, Santa Monica Pier
Building a Better Future Honour Award, 1987 (State of California Department of Rehabilitation Architectural Design Awards Programme) – Carousel Park
City of Santa Monica Mayor's Commendation, October, 1987 – Carousel Park
Excellence on the Waterfront Honour Award, Waterfront Center, 1987 – Carousel Park
American Institute of Architects Honour Award, 1984 – St Matthew's Church
California Council, American Institute of Architects, Merit Award, 1984 – St Matthew's Church
Los Angeles Chapter, American Institute of Architects, Merit Award, 1984 – St Matthew's Church
Architectural Record House of the Year, 1981 – Rodes House
First Prize, Santa Monica Pier Design Charrette, 1981
First Prize, Tegel Harbour International Design Competition, West Berlin, 1980 – Housing, Recreational and Cultural Center
Exhibition, Max Protech Gallery, NYC 1980 – St Matthew's Church
'Contemporary Views of the House', Mandeville Gallery, University of California San Diego, 1983
'The California Condition', La Jolla Museum of Contemporary Art, 1982
'Houses and Cities', Bernard Johnson Gallery, Los Angeles, 1982
'Late Entries to the Tribune Competition', drawing exhibited in Centre Pompidou, Paris, St Louis Art Museum, Museum of Contemporary Art, Chicago, 1977
2nd Prize, Competition for Cultural Center for Plateau Beaubourg with team of Moshe Safdie, Architect, 1971
Alpha Ro Chi Medal, Yale School of Architecture, 1972
Fellow, Branford College, Yale University

Selected Work
Playa Vista Master Plan, Los Angeles, California, in progress
Escondido Cultural Center, Escondido, California, in progress
Kobe Nishiokamoto Housing, Kobe, Japan, in progress
Yudell/Beebe House, Malibu, California, 1989

School of Business Administration, University of California, Berkeley, California, in progress
Boxenbaum Arts Education Centre, Crossroads School, Santa Monica, California, 1989
University of Oregon Science Facilities, Eugene, Oregon, 1989
Humboldt Library, Berlin, West Germany, 1989
St Louis Art Museum, West Wing Restoration and New Decorative Art Galleries, 1989
San Antonio Art Institute, San Antonio, Texas, 1988
Tegel Harbour Housing, Berlin, West Germany, 1987
Tegel Harbour Master Plan, Berlin, West Germany, 1980 to present
Carousel Park, Santa Monica Pier, Santa Monica, California, 1986
King Studio, Artist's Studio and Residence, 1985
Kwee Residence, Republic of Singapore, 1984
University of California, Office of the President, 1984 (project)
St Matthew's Church, Pacific Palisades, California, 1983
The Parador Resort Hotel, San Juan Capistrano, California, 1981 (project)
Rodes Residence, Seal Beach, California, 1979 (project)
County Federal Savings, Stamford, Connecticut, 1976 to 1977
Campus Plan, Hotchkiss School, Lakeville, Connecticut, with Evans Woolen Associates, 1973
Resort Development, St. Simons Island, Georgia, with Charles W Moore Associates, 1972

SELECTED FIRM AWARDS

California Council, American Institute of Architects, Firm of the Year Award, 1992
California Council, American Institute of Architects, Honour Award, 1992 – Yudell/Beebe House, Malibu, California
California Council, American Institute of Architects, Urban Design Award, 1992 – Plaza Las Fuentes, Pasadena, California
American Library Association/AIA Library Building Award, 1991 – Humboldt Library
San Diego Chapter, American Institute of Architects, Honour Award, 1991 – Nativity Catholic Church
Sunset Magazine Western Home Award, 1991 – Yudell/Beebe House
California Council, American Institute of Architects, Honour Award, 1991 – First Church of Christ, Scientist, Glendale

American Wood Council Wood Design Honour Award, 1990 – First Church of Christ, Scientist, Glendale
Los Angeles Chapter, American Institute of Architects, Honour Award, 1990 – Humboldt Library
California Council, American Institute of Architects, Merit Award, 1989 – Anawalt House
American Institute of Architects National Honour Award, 1988 – Tegel Harbour Housing
California Council, American Institute of Architects, Honour Award, 1988 – Tegel Harbour Housing
California Council, American Institute of Architects, Honour Award, 1988 – Carousel Park, Santa Monica Pier
California Department of Rehabilitation, Building a Better Future Honour Award, 1987 – Carousel Park
City of Santa Monica Mayor's Commendation, October, 1987 – Carousel Park
Excellence on the Waterfront Honour Award, Waterfront Center, 1987 – Carousel Park
American Institute of Architects National Honour Award, 1984 – St Matthew's Church
California Council, American Institute of Architects, Merit Award, 1984 – St Matthew's Church
Los Angeles Chapter, American Institute of Architects, Merit Award, 1984 – St Matthew's Church
First Prize, Santa Monica Pier Design Charrette, 1981
First Prize, Tegel Harbour International Design Competition, West Berlin – 1980 Housing, Recreational and Cultural Center

SELECTED PROJECTS
Institutional Work

University of Washington Chemistry Building, Seattle, Washington
All Saints Episcopal Church North Quadrangle, Pasadena, California
Business Administration Building, University of California, Berkeley, California
Powell Library Renovation, University of California, Los Angeles
Bel Air Presbyterian Church, Bel Air, California
West Wing Renovations and New Decorative Arts Galleries, St Louis Art Museum, St Louis, Missouri
San Antonio Art Institute, San Antonio, Texas
Humboldt Library, Berlin, West Germany
Boxenbaum Arts Education Centre, Crossroads School, Santa Monica, California

First Church of Christ, Scientist, Glendale, California
University of Oregon Science Facilities, Eugene, Oregon
Church of the Nativity, Rancho Santa Fe, California
Molecular Biology Research Facility, University of California, San Diego, California
St Matthew's Church, Pacific Palisades, California

Civic and Commercial Projects

Plaza Las Fuentes (Hotel, Offices, Retail, Public Gardens), Pasadena, California
Escondido Cultural Center, Escondido, California
Tegel Harbour Cultural Center, Berlin, West Germany
Carousel Park, Santa Monica Pier, Santa Monica, California
Parador Hotel (Project), San Juan Capistrano, California

Master Planning and Housing

Playa Vista Master Plan, Los Angeles, California
Kobe Nishiokamoto Master Plan and Housing, Kobe, Japan
Sundsterrassen Master Plan and Housing, Malmo, Sweden
Escondido Cultural Center Master Plan, Escondido, California
Tegel Harbour Master Plan, Housing, Cultural Center, and Promenade, Berlin, West Germany
1992 Columbian World Exposition (Project), Chicago, Illinois
Ocean Park Master Plan and Beach Improvements, Santa Monica, California
University of Oregon Science Facilities Master Plan, Eugene, Oregon
San Juan Capistrano Historic District Master Plan and Architectural Guidelines, San Juan, Capistrano, California
Restoration Plan, Seal Beach, California
Sea Ranch Condominium No 1, Sea Ranch, California

Residential Work

Rodes House, Los Angeles, California
Kwee House, Republic of Singapore
King Studio, Los Angeles, California
Inman House, Atlanta, Georgia
Pynoos House, Beverley Hills, California
Anawalt House, Malibu, California
Donaldson House, Santa Monica, California
Yudell/Beebe House, Malibu, California

Charles Moore

John Ruble

Buzz Yudell

NOTE FROM THE ARCHITECTS

We wish to express our appreciation to the staff of Academy Editions for their great care and perseverance in the preparation of this Monograph. The Director, John Stoddart, the Editor, Iona Spens, and the Designer, Andrea Bettella, have collaborated with exceptional energy and professionalism to give coherence and clarity to the presentation of a varied body of work. We are greatly appreciative of James Steele's considerable talents and initiative in efforts in organising and writing significant pieces of this Monograph. James Mary O'Connor, one of our Senior Project Architects, has worked with enormous devotion and in close collaboration with James Steele to see this book realised. Finally, the work presented here is only as successful as our collaboration with the members of our office and the numerous clients and communities with whom we have tried to develop places together.

Charles Moore   John Ruble   Buzz Yudell